CZECHOSLOVAKIA'S COLD WAR REFUGEE CHILDREN

Miriam Potocky Rafaidus

CZECHOSLOVAKIA'S COLD WAR REFUGEE CHILDREN

Contemporary Resonance

The Forced Migration Studies Collection

Collection Editors

T. Alexander Aleinikoff
& Laura Hammond

LPp

First published in 2025 by Lived Places Publishing

British Library Cataloguing in Publication Data
A CIP record for this book is available from the British Library.

ISBN: 9781915734686 (pbk)
ISBN: 9781915734709 (ePDF)
ISBN: 9781915734693 (ePUB)

Cover design by Fiachra McCarthy
Book design by Rachel Trolove of Twin Trail Design
Typeset by Newgen Publishing, UK

Lived Places Publishing
P.O. Box 1845
47 Echo Avenue
Miller Place, NY 11764

www.livedplacespublishing.com

In loving memory of
Vlastimila Potocká (Vlastimila Kutílková)
(1925–2013)
Pavel Potocký (Ruben Auerbach)
(1924–2003)
Asaf Auerbach
(1928–2022)
and
To
Michael J. Potocky (Jan Potocký)

What has been will be again; what has been done will
be done again.

—Ecclesiastes 1:9

Abstract

What can the lived experiences of Czechoslovak Cold War refugee children tell us about the lifetime impact of childhood forced migration? This is the story of the author and over thirty other Czechoslovak Cold War refugee children. The author shares her lived experience, as well as archival oral histories, to ultimately answer the question: does anyone ever stop being a refugee?

Engaging with themes such as memory, trauma, and ethnic identity, these testimonies from some of the earliest and youngest refugees in contemporary history will illuminate an underexamined group and explore what lessons can be learned, applying to refugee children and youth of today and tomorrow.

Key words

lived experience, gerontology, oral history, ethnic identity, trauma, childhood, forced migration, memory, Czechoslovakia, Cold War, Holocaust

Acknowledgments

My gratitude is extended to the National Czech & Slovak Museum & Library, which developed and archived the extraordinary oral history project, *Recording Voices & Documenting Memories of Czech & Slovak Americans*. I am especially indebted to Dr Cecilia Rokusek, President and CEO, and David Muhlena, Library Director. I thank all the participants who shared their stories and hope I have done them justice. All proceeds from this book will benefit the National Czech & Slovak Museum & Library (www.ncsml.org).

I also thank the esteemed editors of this *Forced Migration Series*, Professors T. Alexander Aleinikoff and Laura Hammond, for their steadfast support of this project and for their insightful editorial feedback throughout. I am most grateful to David Parker, co-founder and publisher of Lived Places Publishing, for helping open up publishing to underrepresented voices and for serving as my accountability partner.

Dr Gail Ukockis has stood by me as I have lived this story for nearly half a century.

My husband, David Martin Rafaidus, is my tireless cheerleader and companion explorer of Czechoslovak history and heritage.

Contents

Learning objectives

The aims of this book are to help readers:

1. Understand the reasons for Czechoslovak forced migration during the Cold War.
2. Realize how Cold War political interests shaped refugee policy and the downstream effects for today's refugees.
3. Recognize the psychosocial impacts of childhood forced migration throughout the life span.
4. Identify similarities and differences between Czechoslovak Cold War refugee children and youth and those from other times and places.
5. Apply lessons learned from these voices from the past to tackle today's global refugee crisis.

Foreword

In this book Dr. Miriam Potocky Rafaidus provides amazing insight into the realities of human development and existence during war, dictatorship, and the years beyond. She has brilliantly organized a poignant narrative that resonates deeply with the human experience—especially the experiences of children caught in such turmoil and its aftereffects. This book is not just a story, or series of stories; it is a testament to resilience, identity, and the indomitable spirit of youth that struggles for identity in a critical time of development.

This book is a must read for historians, sociologists, human development specialists, and everyone with an interest and passion to understand the unspoken tragedies of human conflict and dictatorship. This book is extremely timely now at this time in human history as it examines the impacts of war on human development and assimilation that may last a lifetime. War and dictatorship are devastating forces that shatter human life and uproot families. But perhaps the most vulnerable among those affected are the children. They are silent witnesses to chaos, the innocent bystanders in a world turned upside down. Children in their developmental years can be impacted for a lifetime.

This book sheds light on harrowing refugee journeys, with a focus on children who are forced to confront the unimaginable, relocation in a totally foreign land. Through their eyes, one can see and feel the loss of innocence, the abrupt end of childhood, and the heavy burden of survival. Dr. Potocky Rafaidus has captured this in her writing. Once you start reading her brilliant work, you cannot put the book down. As you turn the pages, you will feel and visualize these young souls as they escaped the clutches of violence and destruction not understanding why. Their stories are filled with fear, uncertainty, and hope. They embark on treacherous journeys, leaving behind everything they know, their homes, friends, and familiar sights. This is most difficult for children during their elementary school developmental ages. Each step they take is a testament to their courage, a fight for a chance at a better life. This book captures the essence of that struggle at a point in their lives when they were at the most critical time in their development and individual identity.

Escaping war or dictatorship is only the beginning. The journey does not end with the crossing of borders; it transforms into a new challenge—acclimating to a new country. For these children, the unfamiliar landscapes, languages, and cultures can be overwhelming and continue into their adult lives and even throughout their entire lives.

This book beautifully illustrates the experiences of those who left then-Czechoslovakia. The individual stories illustrate how these children navigated the new world that was filled with both opportunities and obstacles. It highlights the kindness of strangers, the warmth of new friendships, and the bittersweet nostalgia for a homeland left behind. As the children settled into their new lives, they grappled with the complex task of establishing their identities. Who are they in this new land? How do they reconcile their past with their present? This book poignantly explores the struggle of claiming identity amidst the backdrop of history. It captures the essence of growing up as a child in a foreign land, where every day was a step towards self-discovery and acceptance. This book is not just a narrative of survival; it is a celebration of resilience, hope, and the power of identity. It reminds us that while war and dictatorship may take away our homes, it cannot take away our spirit and determination. As we reflect on the stories within these pages, let us remember the children of war and honor their journeys. Thanks to Dr. Potocky Rafaidus for bringing these stories to us and most importantly for examining the developmental hypothesis that the effects of war, displacement, and identity can have on children for a lifetime.

Cecilia Rokusek, Ed.D., M.Sc., RDN
President & CEO
National Czech & Slovak Museum & Library
Cedar Rapids, Iowa, USA

1
A childhood disrupted

A journey through forced migration and identity

It all began for me nearly sixty years ago. One morning in my first-grade class, parents started arriving early to take their children home. This was highly unusual, as parents normally didn't come until much later in the day. No one explained what was happening, and one by one, my classmates left until I was one of the last children remaining. Then my mother arrived and took me home. She didn't say why. On the way, I heard nonstop chatter over the public address loudspeakers strung on lampposts throughout the city. I couldn't understand what was being said.

That evening, my parents, my grandmother, my younger brother, and I were at home when we heard a deep, mechanical, rumbling growl outside. A rhythmic thump, thump, thump shook the house.

My father peered out the window, then quickly turned off all the lights in the house and told my brother and me to crawl under the kitchen table. I asked what it was. He said a row of tanks was rolling down our street.

This was Prague, and this was 1968. The Prague Spring had just been crushed, and my life was about to change.

A few months later, my brother and I were asleep one night when suddenly the lights came on, and my father was in the room. We were going on an airplane ride, he said. Two suitcases were packed and waiting by the door. As we stood at the door, my grandmother draped a gold chain and pendant around my mother's neck as my mother cried.

I wouldn't see Czechoslovakia again for over 25 years. Like hundreds of thousands of others, we were fleeing Communism. A few months later, we arrived in the United States. After a year in New York City, we settled in Denver.

Growing up as both a Czech and an American posed many challenges. At school and in the outside world, I was expected to be like any other American child, but at home, my family tried to maintain Czech traditions. My mother often spoke bitterly about how the Czechoslovak people had been wronged by history. A cloud always hung over the household.

I lived in two worlds, often in conflict. I didn't fully identify as Czech or American. I wasn't even sure what either identity meant. Throughout my childhood and adolescence, I often fantasized about what life might have been like had we stayed in Czechoslovakia. As is the nature of fantasies, I imagined it would have been better. I sought out anything Czechoslovak. But in Denver in the 1970s, that was hard to find. Back then,

Czechoslovakia was shrouded in mystery behind the Iron Curtain, which was practically impenetrable.

Items and news from Czechoslovakia were rare. Although my mother regularly received letters from home (whose stamps I would gaze at for hours), trans-Atlantic phone calls were unheard of. Even if we could afford them, most of our relatives in Prague didn't have phones, and those who did risked political retribution for talking with people in the West. For decades, the land I was born in seemed incredibly distant and unreachable.

I always knew that there must be others out there who shared my experiences, but I never encountered them until I found the oral history archives at the National Czech & Slovak Museum & Library. This collection contains more than 300 recorded inter-views with people who left Czechoslovakia during the Cold War and eventually settled in North America (New York, Washington, D.C., Cleveland, Chicago, San Francisco, Montréal, and Toronto). Among these were the narratives of 33 people whose families, like mine, fled Czechoslovakia when they were children during the Cold War (1948–1989). These people were interviewed dec-ades later (2009–2013), providing a unique view of childhood forced migration from the perspective of mid- to late life.

In the original project, each respondent participated in a 1–3 hour video-recorded interview about their life course, includ-ing early childhood, family history, migration experience, accul-turation experience, and adulthood. For this project, I applied interpretive phenomenological analysis to explore the forced migration experience from each participant's unique perspec-tive, the personal meanings they attached to those experiences, and how those experiences and interpretations impacted their life course. I conducted a close reading of each interview transcript, identified, described, and organized overarching themes in the oral histories, and selected illustrative quotations for each theme. I summarized themes and edited all content for clarity and readability with the aid of generative artificial intelligence (ChatGPT-4o).

I draw upon my own lived experience and these 33 oral histories, as well as archival records, academic publications, literary nonfiction, and fiction to explore a collective childhood forced migration experience and its impacts throughout the life course. Most of us who shared this collective experience are now gone. The rest are in the winter of our lives. This is our story.

Childhood forced migration and human development

The experience of children in refugee families is profoundly different from that of adults. According to sociologist Rubén Rumbaut (2004), childhood migration can be divided into three stages, each affecting adaptation differently. Children who migrate in early childhood (ages 0–5) usually don't remember much, if anything, about their birth country. They can't read or write in their native language because they were too young to go to school there. They pick up the new country's language without an accent and are mostly socialized in the new environment. Rumbaut calls this group the 1.75 generation because their experience is similar to that of U.S.-born second-generation children.

The next group is children who arrive in middle childhood (ages 6–12), known as the classic 1.5 generation. These children have learned, or started to learn, to read and write in their native language at school but finish their education in the new country. The last group is adolescents (ages 13–17) who arrive and either go to secondary school or start working right away. They are the 1.25 generation, whose adaptation is similar to that of adult refugees.

In this book, I suggest that childhood forced migration has lasting effects throughout life. These impacts might even be stronger than those experienced by adults because childhood migration happens during critical developmental stages. This idea is supported by extensive research showing that harmful experiences in childhood have lifelong consequences (Boullier and Blair, 2018). One of the aims of this book is to show how these ideas play out in the real-life stories of Czechoslovakia's Cold War refugee children.

The Cold War and Czechoslovakia

The Cold War was the defining ideological battle of the second half of the twentieth century, fought between the United States and the Soviet Union. The U.S. championed free-market capitalism and democracy, while the Soviet Union pushed for a centrally planned socialist economy and totalitarian rule. Countries around the world ended up aligning with one side or the other, either by choice or by force. Both superpowers had enough nuclear weapons to destroy the planet, so they avoided direct military conflict. Instead, they fought proxy wars, supporting opposing sides in civil wars and coups in countries like Korea, Vietnam, and many in Africa and Latin America. Espionage and propaganda were also major aspects of the Cold War, with the U.S. and the Soviet Union spying on each other and their own citizens. To understand the Cold War's impact on Czechoslovakia, we need to start with the nation's origins. Following is a brief history (Palovic and Bereghazyova, 2020).

Czechoslovakia became an independent democratic republic in 1918, after the First World War. Before that, it was part of the Austro-Hungarian Empire. The new country quickly became the world's tenth-strongest economy and one of its most industrially advanced nations. But this period of freedom and prosperity only lasted twenty years.

In 1938, Czechoslovakia's allies, Great Britain and France, signed the Munich Agreement with Hitler, forcing Czechoslovakia to give up the Sudetenland—a border region with a majority ethnic German population—to Germany. Czechoslovakia had no say in this deal. Britain and France hoped to appease Hitler and avoid war, but instead, they sacrificed Czechoslovakia. Germany then occupied the Sudetenland, forcibly displacing ethnic Czechs. Six months later, Hitler invaded the remaining Czech lands, declaring them a protectorate of the German Reich. The Slovak lands became a puppet state of Germany.

The democratically elected leaders of Czechoslovakia fled and set up two governments in exile: one in London and the other in Moscow. Klement Gottwald, the head of the former Communist Party of Czechoslovakia, led the Moscow faction.

While in Moscow, Stalin personally groomed Gottwald to be his puppet in Czechoslovakia after the war. As the war in Europe was ending in 1945, Stalin, Churchill, and Roosevelt met at the Yalta Conference to decide how to divide the territories. They agreed that the Soviet Union, not the U.S. and Britain, would liberate Czechoslovakia and Eastern Europe, paving the way for Soviet domination in the region.

After the Soviets liberated Czechoslovakia, the Slovak Nazi collaborationist president was arrested, tried, and executed for treason. Czechoslovakia was reunified, and its leadership returned from exile. With Europe in economic ruin, Czechoslovakia's working and middle classes were disillusioned with capitalism and looking for alternatives. In the first post-war election, the Communist Party won the most votes, and Klement Gottwald became the prime minister. Under Stalin's influence, Gottwald used police control, coercion, and intimidation to seize control in a coup in February 1948. The country turned into a communist dictatorship for the next forty years.

The Communist Party quickly enacted harsh social, political, and economic transformations. The borders were closed, isolating Czechoslovakia from the West and essentially imprisoning its people. All media, including news and art, were censored to align with communist ideology. Those who opposed the regime were subjected to staged show trials with fabricated charges and false testimonies, resulting in political imprisonments, forced labor camps, life sentences, and executions. By the early 1950s, there were 422 labor camps and prisons in Czechoslovakia holding over 15,000 political prisoners. By 1960, 4,500 people had died during interrogations and imprisonments, and 248 had been sentenced to death for political "crimes." The rest of the population faced routine harassment through street checks, house searches, and constant surveillance by neighbors, coworkers, and family members, terrorizing most people into submission.

Private property was abolished, and all businesses were seized and nationalized. Family farms were turned into large collectives, forcing farmers to give up their land, equipment, and livestock. Those who resisted were imprisoned or killed. In Slovakia, rapid industrialization destroyed the traditional rural lifestyle. The regime also tried to eliminate religion, seeing it as a threat to its power. Catholic priests, members of religious orders, and Jewish Party leaders were prosecuted and sometimes executed. Monasteries and convents were shut down, and people were punished for attending religious services.

After both Stalin and Gottwald died in 1953, the communist grip in Eastern and Central Europe started to loosen very slowly. In Czechoslovakia, this political and social thaw led to the Prague Spring of 1968, led by Alexander Dubček, the head of the Czechoslovak Communist Party. Dubček aimed to create what he called "socialism with a human face," allowing more freedom of speech, press, and travel abroad. The Soviet Union, fearing it might lose one of its most industrialized satellite countries, was not happy. On the night of August 20–21, 1968, the Soviet Union, Hungary, Poland, East Germany, and Bulgaria invaded Czechoslovakia with over 250,000 troops, several thousand tanks, and hundreds of aircraft. The invasion resulted in over 100 deaths and 500 injuries. All the Prague Spring reforms were reversed, Dubček was forced to resign, and a Kremlin loyalist took over. This marked the start of the so-called "normalization" period, which meant a return to political purges, imprisonments, and widespread repression.

In 1985, Mikhail Gorbachev was elected General Secretary by the Communist Party of the Soviet Union. He kicked off a series of reforms to revive the stagnant Soviet economy and to loosen the totalitarian grip across the Soviet Union and its satellite states. By late 1989, revolutionary changes swept through Eastern and Central Europe, stunning the world. On November 9, 1989, protesters from both East and West tore down the Berlin Wall, the most potent symbol of the Cold War.

On November 17, a massive student-led demonstration in Prague sparked a weeklong protest with nightly demonstrations across the country. Leading the revolution was Václav Havel, a prominent playwright, dissident, and political prisoner. On November 24, the entire Communist Party leadership in Czechoslovakia resigned. On December 29, Václav Havel was democratically elected the new president. The Cold War was over.

Czechoslovak forced migration during the Cold War

The oppressive totalitarian regime left people with a few tough choices: join the Party and benefit from your connections; keep your head down and avoid trouble; speak out and face harassment, imprisonment, or execution; or try to escape to the West. It's estimated that more than a half-million people, or about 3.5 per cent of the total population, fled the country during the Cold War (1948–1989) (Kopanic, 2022). In the process of escape, about

300 people died by gunshot, explosion, electrocution, or drowning over this 40-year period (Palovic and Bereghazyova, 2020).

This forced migration mainly occurred in two major waves, following the political crises in 1948 and 1968. About 60,000 people fled between 1948 and 1950. These were political and thought leaders whose lives were in immediate danger after the communist coup, as well as people whose factories or agricultural properties were seized by the Communists. The second large wave followed the Soviet-led invasion in August 1968. Over the next two months, about 104,000 people fled. Many again came from the educated segments of society, including a significant number of professionals and thought leaders who had become disillusioned with the Party (Kopanic, 2022). Many were young adults who happened to be abroad when the August 21 invasion occurred, thanks to the easing of travel restrictions during the Prague Spring. They applied for asylum where they were, becoming what I call "accidental refugees." Others crossed borders by car or motorcycle during the chaos of that day and those that followed.

After 1968, politically motivated emigration steadily continued at a rate of about 5,000 annually. By the 1980s, the rate rose to about 10,000 per year. Many exited to the West via travel to Yugoslavia, where the borders remained relatively open. In total, starting in 1968, about 250,000 Czechs and Slovaks had emigrated to the West by 1989 (Kopanic, 2022).

These refugees resettled primarily in the United States and Canada (other resettlement countries included Western European nations, the United Kingdom, Israel, Australia, and

New Zealand). The U.S. and Canada granted them refugee status because it served their geopolitical and economic interests of winning the Cold War (Raska, 2012; Zolberg, 1988). Part of the strategy was that the refugees would serve as symbols in anti-Communist propaganda.

Before the end of the Second World War, international law didn't differentiate between economic immigrants and refugees fleeing persecution. In the United States, President Truman issued a Directive on Displaced Persons in 1945, expediting the admission of Holocaust survivors living in displaced persons camps throughout Europe. This was followed by the Displaced Persons Act of 1948, allowing the admission of many Czechoslovak refugees from the 1948 wave who had escaped to those camps. The law required that admitted displaced persons find housing and a job that wouldn't replace an existing worker in the United States.

The Refugee Relief Act of 1953 authorized over 200,000 visas for refugees from Communist countries. To be eligible, refugees had to provide evidence of a guaranteed home and job from a U.S. resident, secure sponsorship from a U.S. citizen, prove their opposition to communism, and pay for their travel costs. The Migration and Refugee Assistance Act of 1962 provided monetary assistance to refugees fleeing communist countries during the Cold War (U.S. Citizenship and Immigration Service, 2023). After the Soviet invasion of Czechoslovakia in 1968, President Johnson ordered provisions for the entry of Czechoslovak refugees, allocating funds for their reception, care, resettlement, transportation, and integration. Finally, in 1980, responding to the Vietnamese refugee crisis that began with the fall of Saigon to Communist forces, the United States enacted the Refugee Act of 1980, its first comprehensive refugee legislation, which remains in effect today. A similar series of ad-hoc admissions policies in response to Cold War refugees happened in Canada (Raska, 2018).

Summary and conclusions

In this introductory chapter, we have explored how childhood forced migration differs from adulthood. We have seen that Czechoslovakia's history from 1918 to 1989 was marked by significant political upheaval, including Nazi occupation and a Soviet-led communist regime and military invasion. These events created a climate of fear and repression, driving waves of forced migration. Western countries, particularly the United States, granted refugee status to Czechoslovaks largely due to geopolitical interests. This support served as a propaganda tool against communism, illustrating how international politics shape humanitarian policies.

This overview shows the complex interplay of historical events, individual experiences, and policy decisions in shaping the lived experiences of refugee children. We see that Czechoslovaks were among the first recognized political refugees in modern post-Second World War history. We, their children, have among the longest post-resettlement lived experiences in modern Western history. It is my hope that reflecting on these experiences of past refugees can provide valuable insights for current and future refugee crises.

2
Echoes of home
Childhood memories before displacement

My family's house in Modřany, in Prague's District 4, was situated on the edge of a forest. My father used to take me there in the summers to hunt mushrooms. In my memory, all the details of these walks are perfectly preserved: sunlight streaking through the treetops, glinting on leaves; a stream bubbling; damp rising from the forest floor. These sights, sounds, and smells form my most vivid memory of my homeland.

Introduction

In this chapter, we journey back to recollections of our childhoods in Czechoslovakia. Before the upheaval of forced migration, our lives were deeply intertwined with the places we called home, the people who nurtured us, and the natural landscapes that shaped our daily experiences. These memories, etched into our consciousness, provide a window into a time that was both idyllic and formative.

As we delve into these memories, we confront the shadow of war and political upheaval that loomed over our early years.

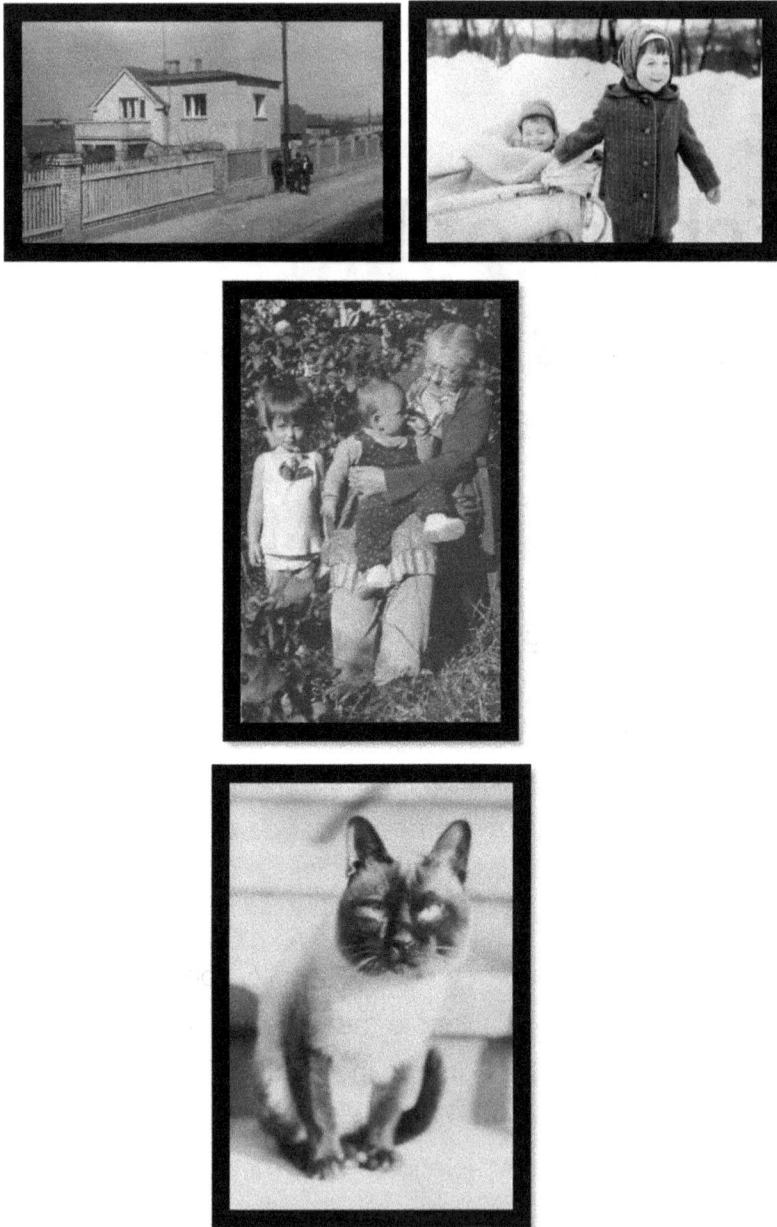

Figure 1 Happy childhood: The family home in Prague; the author with her brother in the snow and in the garden with grandma, c. 1965; the family cat, Míša.

The traumatic events of the Second World War and the subsequent Communist revolution disrupted our idyllic childhoods. Through personal narratives and shared memories, we begin to uncover the impact of our formative years on our sense of self and belonging.

Early childhood

The participants' early childhood memories often reveal a deep connection to their specific places of origin, with many, like me, identifying exact neighborhoods, towns, or even street addresses when recalling their birthplaces. This precise identification underscores the significance of our early environments and the strong emotional ties we hold to these locations. These stories illustrate how, despite displacement and the passage of time, the specific geographic origins of our early lives remain deeply ingrained in our identities and memories.

> I lived in the Strašnice area, that's Prague 10.
>
> —Pavel, displaced at less than 1 year, 1950

> I was born in a small town outside of Bratislava, Stupava.
>
> —Valentin, displaced at 14 in 1952

> I lived on 33 Rajsková Street. That address is forever etched into my memory because it was a really lovely time of my life.
>
> —Paulina, displaced at 8 in 1973

The natural environment seems to loom large in our memories. Recollections of farming, walking in the woods, mushroom hunting, berry picking, frog-catching, and fishing were shared by numerous participants.

> We had a forest preserve behind the house, so I would love to go out there and ride a bike and go fishing. We spent a lot of time in the country as well. My parents had a cottage, an old 1600s inn that was converted into a house.
>
> —Luke, displaced at 9 in 1980

Is nature so prominent in others' childhood memories? Or is this something more elemental—Mother Earth connecting us back to our roots?

> I was like a flower ripped up by its roots with dirt still hanging onto it.
>
> —Jerri, displaced at less than 1 in 1949

Our earliest memories have an idyllic, nostalgic quality. Perhaps this is something we subconsciously superimpose on our past because our actual early memories are unreliable. For those, such as myself, who left Czechoslovakia before adolescence, most of our knowledge and views about the country came from our parents. I often cannot distinguish between my own lived memories, and those absorbed from my parents, an experience I sense may be shared by some of my cohorts.

> Everything kind of rubs together. It's hard to distinguish.
>
> —Ivana, displaced at 3 in 1949

> I remember a sense of Prague. I remember Prague in contrast.
>
> —Yvette, displaced at 10 in 1968

War

The older children displaced in the 1948 wave often carried vivid recollections of the Second World War, highlighting the profound impact the conflict had on their early lives. These memories are marked by the brutality and chaos of war, underscoring the deep and lasting scars left by the war on these children, shaping their experiences and perspectives as they navigated subsequent displacement and resettlement.

> They used to bring truckloads of German dead bodies that they executed for desertions and dumped them. I saw Russian prisoners being marched through town under German guard and they looked bad. They were starving. Toward the end of the war, a drunken Russian soldier right by our house fell and hit his head on a cobblestone and cracked it open. An officer came over, looked at him, and shot him.
>
> —Savoy, displaced at 15 in 1948

> My great-grandfather took me for a walk in 1939 and warned me to obey my parents as terrible things were happening. At three, I followed his advice for years. In 1942, I saw my great-grandfather in a suit with a yellow Star of David. I knew I'd never see him again. Two years later, my mother was sent to a labor camp, and I was hidden on a farm. I later learned I was three-quarters Jewish, though raised Catholic.
>
> —Charles, displaced at 12 in 1948

Social class

The families' living conditions in Czechoslovakia were very different between the two major refugee waves of 1948 and 1968. A large proportion of the 1948 refugee families were the upper-class elite whose livelihoods, and lives, were the targets of the Communist revolution. These included political officials and business and landowners. Among the families included here, political officials included an ambassador, a political party secretary, and a press attaché. The businesses these families were forced to abandon included a perfume shop, a luggage manufacturer, a clothing company, a bicycle factory, a restaurant, a distillery, and a family farm.

Despite the country's overall economic hardship after the war, some of these children appeared to live in relative comfort.

> On the farm there were chickens, geese, and ducks so we always had enough to eat.
>
> —Rudolf, displaced at 13 in 1948

> My father was in the foreign ministry. My parents had a fabulous apartment by the castle.
>
> —Madeleine, displaced at 11 in 1948

The Communist system purported to create a classless society. Consequently, although the families of 1968 and later included a fair number of educated workers such as health care providers, professors, and artists, they were not the country's elite (those were now Party leaders from the former working class). By 1968, this group had lived for two decades under Communist oppression and its economic scarcity.

I grew up in an efficiency apartment in Prague 2. The bathroom was in the hallway. We had a wood-burning stove. We didn't have fresh fruit unless it was Christmas, when we got tangerines. I can still smell them.

—Yvette, displaced at 10 in 1968

You wouldn't buy everything in one store. You had a store for vegetables, a store for bread, a store for groceries. We'd go to the store and one of us goes in line to buy potatoes, the other one goes in line to buy bread, the third one goes to buy meat, and mom would go to the regular grocery store to buy everything else.

—Emil, displaced at 15 in 1969.

Relatives from the States sent us an occasional check for about 50 bucks. You would exchange that for this special currency which you could use at a special store where you could buy stuff that you couldn't get anywhere else—Nestlé chocolate milk, foreign cigarettes, instant coffee, Beatles records.

—George G., displaced at 15 in 1968.

My parents were what capitalism calls the working class. They both worked in an electrical parts factory. My mother was a secretary and my father, a mechanic. The four of us lived with my mother's mother in a large, two-story house. The house had electricity, plumbing, and a vegetable and flower garden. We were a few blocks from the Vltava River, where we swam in the summers.

Communist ideology

The narratives of those who attended school in Czechoslovakia during the Cold War reveal the pervasive and often absurd nature of Communist indoctrination. Students were exposed to Russian propaganda from a young age, learning songs and poems that extolled the virtues of the Soviet system. Children's probing questions were met with cautious responses from adults, highlighting the fear of dissent and the gradual, disillusioning revelation of the regime's crimes.

> We were taught a lot of Russian propaganda, a lot of Russian songs. We left when I was in third grade, but already by that time I had won a contest in which I recited a Russian poem. I won a Russian pen that never worked. My aspiration of my life was to be a Pioneer and go see Lenin's grave.
>
> —Paulina, displaced at 8 in 1973

> When I asked questions, people were hesitant to answer, always promoting the greatness of the Soviet system. Things changed in the mid-'60s; suddenly, a teacher admitted, "Stalin isn't on the good list because he had some of his own people shot." It was shocking—a first hint that the Soviet Union wasn't as perfect as we'd been told.
>
> —Vaclav, displaced at 13 in 1969

The absurdity of life under Communism is illustrated in anecdotes that could serve as archetypal examples of Communist-era humor. At the same time, these stories illustrate the resignation of the powerless to the omnipotent system.

Every apartment building had a Party-member care-taker, usually living on the ground floor to watch every-one. My father, an upright, good-looking man, caught the attention of our caretaker, who got everyone to sign a petition against his "arrogant" walk and not greeting neighbors. Exhausted from 18-hour shifts, he may have missed a greeting, but not out of dislike. He then had to defend himself in a residents' meeting over this.

—Vladimir, displaced at 16 in 1968.

As conductor of the Northern Czech Symphony Orchestra, my father had to attend long commu-nist meetings in Teplice. The orchestra would play the Czechoslovak, Russian, and Internationale anthems at the start and end, forcing them to sit through hours of discussions. When my father suggested using a record-ing instead, he was threatened with a coal mine job. So he continued attending.

—Susan, displaced at 14 in 1969

1968 invasion

Those who experienced the Soviet-led occupation of Czechoslovakia in 1968 described a time of fear, tension, and resistance. Their stories capture the sudden, shocking, and palpa-ble nature of the invasion. These eyewitness accounts highlight the pervasive sense of threat and the community's heightened state of fear. The emotional impact of the invasion is summa-rized in a father's reaction to the occupation, emphasizing the deep sense of injustice felt by many. These narratives collectively depict a period marked by upheaval and resistance, as well as the psychological scars left by the occupation.

My father and I were fishing on the Hungarian border and we found out at seven in the morning that Warsaw Pact forces occupied us. We got into the car and drove home. We had a couple uncomfortable experiences where the tanks almost ran us off the road.

—Emil, displaced at 15 in 1969

About a week after the invasion, my father and I went to Wenceslas Square, where things had calmed down. While talking to Russian soldiers, they suddenly started shooting, so we dropped to the ground and crawled to a nearby street. With doors shut in fear, we crawled about a block, turned a corner, and escaped. It was terrifying.

—Susan, displaced at 14 in 1969

When the Russians came on August 21, my dad almost broke down. He said, "There was a terrible injustice done to us this day. Never forget that."

—Vaclav, displaced at 13 in 1969

Summary and conclusions

This chapter explores memories of our childhoods in Czechoslovakia. Many participants in this study, like myself, pin-pointed their origins to specific neighborhoods, villages, or even streets, underscoring a deeply rooted connection to place. Many of us recalled idyllic, nature-filled early childhoods.

For those of us who left Czechoslovakia before adolescence, our understanding of our birthplace was shaped in large part by our parents' stories. Among those who left in infancy, this was entirely the case, as they had no personal recollections. Consequently, in adolescence, our developing sense of identity was intertwined with the narratives we absorbed from our parents.

Those who left in adolescence carried their lived experiences of war and communist oppression, a topic to which we will return in a future chapter. The social class differences between the refugee waves of 1948 and 1968 reflect the shifting political landscape that further shaped our collective experiences.

In conclusion, this chapter begins the examination of the impact of our childhood memories on our life course. The narratives of this pre-departure stage hint at a longing for our native land and desire to reconnect with our roots that remained powerful forces in our lives despite the passage of time and distance.

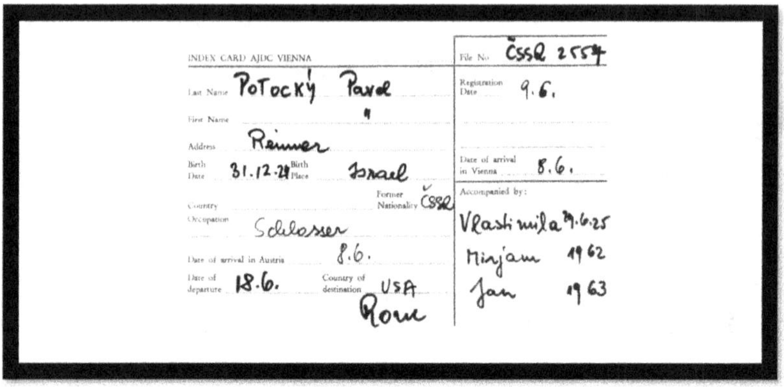

INDEX CARD AJDC VIENNA

File No ČSSR 2554

Last Name POTOCKÝ Pavel

Registration Date 9.6.

First Name "

Address Reimer

Birth Date 31.12.24 Birth Place Israel

Date of arrival in Vienna 8.6.

Country

Former Nationality ČSSR

Accompanied by:

Occupation Schlosser

Vlastimila 29.6.25

Date of arrival in Austria 8.6.

Mirjam 1962

Date of departure 18.6.

Country of destination USA Rome

Jan 1963

Figure 2 Transit: Index card from the AJDC (American Jewish Joint Distribution Committee) showing the family's transit stay in Vienna with a destination of the USA via Rome, 1969.

3
Crossing borders
The journey of displacement

It was our first plane ride. All I remember is that my little brother got sick and had to use a barf bag. We landed in Vienna and took a taxi to a hotel. Suddenly my mother started spewing gibberish with the taxi driver. Strange words came out of her mouth. I stared at her. My mother had turned into an alien.

Introduction

The journey of displacement redefines the contours of life for those forced to flee their homes. In this chapter, we delve into the personal narratives of families escaping the Communist coup in Czechoslovakia, starting with their sudden departures in the wake of political turmoil, traversing the perils of border crossings, and navigating the uncertainties of refugee camps.

This chapter aims to illuminate the psychological and emotional impacts of such a journey and its long-lasting effects on individuals at various stages of their lives. Each narrative offers a window into the complex realities of displacement.

As we explore these personal accounts, we also consider the broader historical and social contexts that shaped their experiences. The refugee camps, though often harsh and dehumanizing, became spaces of community and survival. The final transitions to new countries, marked by both hope and disillusionment, represent the culmination of their journeys and the start of their new lives.

Departure

In the tumultuous aftermath of the Communist takeover in February 1948, many families found themselves facing sudden and perilous decisions. These narratives offer a vivid and personal glimpse into the harrowing experiences these families faced. Each story, while unique in its details, shares common themes of fear, urgency, and the impact of political upheaval on individual lives.

One tale underscores the precarious position of critics in the face of authoritarian regimes, as well as the rapid adjustments families had to make to survive. Another emphasizes the role of personal networks and the stark reality of political purges. We see how families were forced to make rapid decisions, abandon their homes, and rely on both their wits and each other to survive.

> Right after the Communists took over, my father was interrogated because he was a journalist who wrote against communists. He realized that we had to get out. We left almost immediately, in March. We weren't prepared but I guess we got prepared very quickly.
>
> —Barbara, displaced at 13 in 1948

> My father, who was active in the Agrarian Party, was warned by a childhood friend, a Communist Party

member, in April 1948. He told him, "Your name is at the top of the list. The Communists are coming for you tomorrow, planning to send you to Siberia. You need to leave now before they arrive in the morning."

—Jerry, displaced at 3 in 1948

We had to leave everything and walk to the train station late at night, pretending to visit relatives. My father went ahead first, and then my mother, brother, and I followed. The streets were empty and spooky, with no cars. There was a drunk across the street making a lot of noise, which was scary.

—Joan (Jerry's sister), displaced at 7 in 1948

In many cases, fathers who were in immediate danger fled first, intending to pave the way for their families' eventual escape. These family separations highlight the urgency and secrecy required. The coordinated efforts to support and reunite families underscore the complexity, risks, and sacrifices families took to ensure their survival amidst political instability.

In February 1948, I left Prague for a two-week mountain trip to try out new skis, despite my father's concerns about the crisis in Czechoslovakia. With my mother's support, I went, but upon my return, I found my father was gone. Though I continued school, I had to watch what I said. We eventually received a postcard from Chicago in his handwriting, confirming his safety. With help from friends and relatives, we managed to escape ourselves in September 1948.

—Tony, displaced at 14 in 1948

In June 1948, my father was threatened with arrest and often summoned by authorities, but he avoided them. A farmer helped him escape to Paris, leaving my mother, sister, and me behind. In July, my mother received instructions to take us by train to a town near Regensburg, Germany, which we followed.

—Duke, displaced at 8 in 1948

While most of the escapes in the 1948 era were abrupt and clandestine, departures in 1968 and later were more varied. Travel restrictions to the West had loosened in the years leading up to the Prague Spring, and the borders remained relatively fluid until November 1968 (Kopanic, 2022). However, in the days following the August 21 invasion, chaotic escapes and family separations occurred once again.

When armored vehicles rolled down the streets, chaos and shock set in. We were in a limbo until my parents decided it was time to leave, realizing there was nothing left for us. We planned to visit my mother's family in Israel, so I forged an invitation letter from my "ill" grandfather. My mother and I went to get an exit visa, waiting hours in line. I held it together, despite my mother's tears and having to leave our dog behind—a memory that still pains me 43 years later.

—George G., displaced at 15 in 1968

In summer 1968, my parents secured passports and visas to visit an uncle in Austria. On August 21st, at 2 a.m., my cousin called, saying, "We're being occupied." Gunfire sounded on the radio as they urged people to stay calm. I'll never forget seeing my father pacing, uncertain and distressed. Early the next day, he told us to pack up—we were leaving. We weren't sure if we'd ever return. We started driving. My dad was confused and drove in circles a couple of times. It was a huge decision, nerve-racking.

—Dagmar, displaced at 15 in 1968

During the invasion, my parents got on a motorcycle and escaped across the border to Austria. This was a dangerous trip so they didn't want to take a three-year-old with them, so they left me with my grandmother. I wouldn't see my mother for three years and my father for six years.

—Paulina, displaced at 8 in 1973

After 1968, the departure narratives reveal a shift in the nature of escapes from abrupt and clandestine to more planned, yet still secretive endeavors. Families often orchestrated their departures under the guise of vacations, carefully navigating bureaucratic processes and maintaining strict confidentiality to avoid detection by the authorities. Families planned departures while keeping their true intentions hidden from friends and even close relatives. These stories underscore the ongoing tension between the desire for freedom and the constant threat of discovery, illustrating the lengths to which individuals went to secure their futures while managing the emotional toll of such fraught decisions.

My father decided it was time to leave, feeling this was his last chance. He and my mother were careful not to discuss it with anyone, avoiding suspicion. We'd heard of people on vacation in Austria or Yugoslavia who didn't return, but we didn't know anyone planning to leave. My father, a music professor, used a student's planned performance in Salzburg as a reason to get permission for us to travel through Austria. Miraculously, we got permission for a four-day stay. So, on April 17, 1969, we packed up, got in the car, and headed to the southern border.

—Susan, displaced at 14 in 1969

The idea of coming to America began when my mom asked if I'd stay in Czechoslovakia with my dad or leave with her and my stepfather. I chose to go with her, even though I loved both my parents. My mom, who wasn't a Communist Party member, faced issues that led us to plan a "vacation" to Yugoslavia—with no intention of returning. Before we left, she had to visit the police several times, and the secret police even questioned her at work, but they couldn't stop us. I couldn't tell my friends or even my dad, which still makes me feel guilty.

—Alex, displaced at 17 in 1983

Border crossing

Narratives of the 1948 group highlight the perilous and often clandestine nature of their escapes, typically undertaken with the aid of smugglers. These journeys frequently involved crossing rugged terrain on foot. Prominent migration pathways were west through the mountains bordering Germany and south to the western sectors of Vienna (Nekola, 2022). Collectively, these stories underscore the determination of individuals and families risking everything to flee.

> There were about fourteen of us crossing through the mountains. We started on skis, but due to low snow, the smuggler hired by my father told us to leave them and continue on foot. After five hours, we reached a farmhouse around 3 a.m. to rest. By morning, they served us breakfast; we had no baggage, pretending we'd just been out hiking and got lost. At one point, we had to dash across a road while guards changed shifts. Once across, the smuggler told us we could finally relax.
>
> —Barbara, displaced at 13 in 1948

> We took a night train to Plzeň [Pilsen], then transferred to a small village. My mother, two siblings, and I wore casual clothes. Around noon, under cloudy, drizzly skies, we got off the train and walked through the woods for three hours, gathering mushrooms and blueberries to quench our thirst. Eventually, we reached a ravine with a road leading to a wooden gate, thinking it was the border. Carefully, we slid down the slope, worried about being caught. At the bottom, we saw lumberjacks and asked, in broken German, if we were near Germany. They confirmed, pointing us up the road, where we soon met a German border patrol.
>
> —Tony, displaced at 14 in 1948.

By 1968, cars and planes were the most common ways of crossing borders. Recollections from this time reveal the nerve-wracking experiences and strategic planning involved. These accounts illustrate the continued anxiety and uncertainty faced by refugees, as well as the creative strategies they employed to secure their freedom.

> It was nerve-racking heading to West Germany in a convoy of army cars. My mother started panicking, and we did too, seeing soldiers in the woods as we got closer to the border. I remember holding a doll, silent and scared. At one point, a barricade was turning cars back, but my dad found another route up a hill where two soldiers stood. He told them, "We're going to Germany; we have papers." One soldier used a field phone and said, "Clear the way." That day marked the end of life as we knew it.
>
> —Dagmar, displaced at 15 in 1968

> One morning on our front steps, my father suggested we try to go to the U.S. I was 13 and thought it sounded like an adventure, so I agreed. He went to work, and I packed essentials, including a sleeping bag, in case we ended up sleeping on floors. We packed up the car under the pretense of visiting a sick uncle in southern Bohemia. A forester guided us to a small border crossing, then pointed us to continue alone. The border guard looked at our passport and, without the right visa, said, "Better make it quick." We crossed and made it into Austria.
>
> —Paul, displaced at 14 in 1968.

Transit

Following the Second World War, over twenty million people in Europe were displaced, including former Jewish prisoners, forced laborers, expelled German minorities, and those fleeing the Soviet regime. In response, the Allied military forces and the United Nations established displaced persons (DP) camps in the Western-occupied zones of Germany, Austria, and Italy.

In July 1948, the UN granted Czechoslovaks the same political refugee status and protection as other camp residents. By the end of 1948, Czechoslovak refugees were dispersed in over a dozen camps (Nekola, 2022).

Camp accommodations were basic, using wooden shacks, former military barracks, schools, factories, tents, and train cars. Life in the camps was tense due to fears of a potential Cold War conflict between the USA and USSR. Many residents remained for months or years, awaiting visas, work permits, and transport to new homes. The camps were microcosms of society, featuring a mix of community institutions (churches, schools, shops, sports clubs) and illicit activities (prostitution, black markets, communist informants). Political activity also flourished, with some political parties banned in their home countries re-establishing themselves within the camps (Nekola, 2019).

> In the camp we lived in one room shared with two or three other families. The bathroom down the hall was shared by many. It was an old, bombed-out army barracks with rubble everywhere—not a good place for kids. The basements were eerie, and playing there felt awful. The whole experience was tough.
>
> —Duke, displaced at 8 in 1948

Our first camp was a former POW camp in terrible condition. The second was slightly better but still challenging, with 24 people sharing a room, making sleep difficult. In the third camp, we finally had our own room in an old German barracks, which gave us much-needed privacy. We spent time with other refugees, many professionals, discussing politics and hopes for life in America or England. My father learned welding for future work, and I took a carpentry course. A memorable experience was a trip to Nuremberg. The city was in ruins, with walls and chimneys standing amid rubble. I almost felt sorry for the Germans.

—Charles, displaced at 12 in 1948

Most of the families in the circa-1948 wave passed through these camps. Among the others, some were able to travel directly to the West because of pre-existing diplomatic connections. A few were able to obtain visas to emigrate directly to Israel based on their Jewish heritage. In one case, this was forged.

My mother, a press attaché at the Dutch embassy, was under pressure after the Communists identified her boss as a spy. She negotiated with the secret police to leave, with help from the Dutch government. We took a six-week freighter trip from Holland to Australia.

—Thomas, displaced at 8 in 1949

Ironically, my father claimed to be Jewish and used forged documents to say he needed to immigrate to Israel. This allowed him to leave legally with all his property, including his workshop equipment, which he sold in Israel for some capital. His real goal was to reach Canada, but Israel was his chosen route out.

—Ivana, displaced at 3 in 1949.

Camps remained a significant part of Czechoslovak refugees' experiences throughout the Cold War. About half of the families who fled in 1968 or later spent time in these facilities. These camps provided a temporary haven but also introduced new challenges and uncertainties.

> We took a one-hour flight to Vienna and went straight to a refugee camp. At 17, I was considered an adult, so they put me in a special section to check for Communist ties, which terrified my mom. We spent about four months in camps.
>
> —Vladimir, displaced at 17 in 1968.

> The hardest part in Austria was being only 40 minutes from the border, so close to family we couldn't see or talk to. As political asylum seekers, we were safe in the camp but warned against leaving it.
>
> —Petra, displaced at 7 in 1986

> We first lived in a tent on the outskirts of Austria, where my father, who spoke German, quickly found work as a waiter. I remember shivering in the mornings as he shaved inside the tent. We registered with a U.S.-based refugee organization. Then we moved to a hospitality house with cramped conditions, sharing two rooms with other families. My father tried enrolling me in school, but no school would take me for just a few months.
>
> —Vaclav, displaced at 13 in 1969

For some, including myself, the transit experience was largely positive.

We stayed in a guest house in Vienna. My vague impressions of the city revolve around a wedding-cake palace surrounded by vast kaleidoscopic gardens. After a ten-day stay, a refugee assistance agency sent us to Rome, where we spent four months in another guest house with several other Czech refugees.

For a seven-year-old, Rome was an endless adventure. My parents weren't permitted to work while waiting for their visas, so the whole family spent every day exploring the city. With its ancient ruins and vibrant streets, every corner hid a new treasure. I marveled at the Colosseum, imagining lions in the exposed underground passages. I clambered over the fallen columns in the Forum.

The streets bustled with gesticulating people, pint-sized Fiats, and overloaded Vespas. The air was filled with the smells of pizza bianca in osterias and fresh seafood at open-air markets. Street vendors sold olives in newspaper cones. We splashed in every fountain at every piazza. We strolled the cypress-lined Via Appia Antica and the enchanted gardens of Villa Borghese and Villa d'Este. We tasted the salt in the seafoam at Ostia.

I've now lived half my life in Florida, another warm peninsula that clings to the southern end of another continent. Place names like Via and Villa and Villaggio abound here. My home is white stucco with a barrel tile roof. My backyard is filled with hand-painted ceramic tile and pottery. Water cascades in the pool.

Transatlantic passage

Following their stay in camps or other temporary accommo-dations in Germany or Austria, most families traveled directly to North America. In the 1940s, these journeys were made by ship, lasting several days and involving challenging conditions. By the 1960s, airplanes became the standard mode of travel, significantly shortening the journey and altering the transit experience. Despite the changes in transportation methods over the decades, the underlying theme of enduring hardship and uncertainty in pursuit of a safer and more stable future remains constant.

> The ship took seven or eight days to cross the ocean. There were two hulls or two great big dormitories where the sailors had lived, and this is where we stayed for the seven or eight days. The families were separated and segregated. The women were put into one large dorm and the men into another. I believe since I was relatively young, I might have been with my mother, and my father was in a separate room. I remember being seasick as hell. As a matter of fact, I think everybody was.
>
> —Duke, displaced at 8 in 1948

Several of the children underwent multiple displacements before ultimately settling in North America. These stories highlight the varied and often tumultuous paths refugees traversed, involving multiple countries and prolonged periods of uncertainty before finding a permanent residence.

> Living in Israel during its early years was formative and exciting. It was a time of strong nationalism and a push for assimilation among the diverse immigrant population. I felt more connected to the emerging Israeli culture than to my Czech roots during those years. My father

had always dreamed of moving to the United States. After moving to Israel, it took seven years to arrange the paperwork to move to the United States.

—Michlean, displaced at 8 in 1948.

While waiting for immigration approval, we had to choose between Australia and Norway. My mother, terrified of snakes, chose Norway, where we lived for four years. I loved the fjord, mountains, and ocean liners—a beautiful, happy time for me. My mother loved Norway, but my father disliked the cold and socialism. Encouraged by his brother in Canada, he decided we should move to Montréal for better opportunities and more freedom.

—Jerri, displaced at less than 1 in 1949

After my parents escaped to Sweden, I stayed in Czechoslovakia with my grandmother, as they had no way to get me out. They staged a hunger strike outside the Czechoslovak embassy in Stockholm with photos of me, drawing Swedish public and media attention. After three years, with journalists' help, they planned to kidnap me from school, but my mother was caught and placed under house arrest. Eventually, Czechoslovak authorities issued us passports, allowing us to leave when I was eight. My parents divorced shortly after we arrived in Sweden. I spent my teenage years there, then moved to Paris at 15 to model, and came to New York at 17 for *Sports Illustrated*.

—Paulina, displaced at 8 in 1973

Arrival

The initial arrival in a destination country was often a jarring and disorienting experience, marked by feelings of loneliness, cultural shock, and unexpected realities. One narrative recounts the arrival of a young child in Canada, feeling isolated and depressed despite a warm welcome. Another story highlights a teenager's struggle with cultural adjustment in Israel, facing mockery for their appearance. An account of arriving in Chicago reveals a mix of amazement and disappointment at the advanced technology and the stark contrast between expected and actual neighborhoods. Finally, the narrative of a family moving from a small town to Atlanta underscores the alienation and strangeness felt in an urban environment where familiar social dynamics and landscapes were absent.

> We left Norway on a Norwegian ocean liner and arrived in Halifax when I was five and a half. Dressed in a white dress my mother put me in, I saw people waving flags as we landed. Although my uncle was in Montréal, no one met us in Halifax. Immigration arranged for a nun to take us to the train station for Montréal. I felt intensely lonely, experiencing firsthand what it meant to be an immigrant.
>
> —Jerri, displaced at less than 1 in 1949

> We flew to Israel after a month in Vienna. Dressed in jeans and hippie shirts with long hair, I stood out and was mocked for being from Czechoslovakia, seen as backward. I hated it and once tried running to the Austrian

embassy to return, but my father caught me. I struggled with the adjustment, finding that first year very rough.

—George G., displaced at 15 in 1968

We arrived at O'Hare airport in Chicago. We were greeted by some politicians. There was a car with all-leather seats and power windows. It was all new to me. I was surprised and disappointed by some of the neighborhoods. I thought America was all beautiful buildings and high rises, but I saw bad neighborhoods and burned-out buildings.

—Alex, displaced at 17 in 1983

It was a big shock because I was from a small town in the mountains, and suddenly we were in Atlanta, a big city. We couldn't just go out anywhere. Everyone lived in the suburbs. I remember getting all dressed up to go for a walk through Atlanta, but there was nothing to look at and no people around. It was very strange.

—Vaclav, displaced at 13 in 1969

Summary and conclusions

In this chapter, we explored the profound impact of displacement on families fleeing Czechoslovakia during and after the Communist takeovers of 1948 and 1968. The narratives in this chapter detail how families faced perils of escape, border crossings, and life in refugee camps. These stories reveal the impact of fear, urgency, and the need for secrecy. The chapter also examines the broader historical and social contexts that shaped these experiences, including the communal life in refugee camps and the mixed emotions tied to arrival in new countries.

This chapter illustrates that the journey of displacement is not just a physical relocation but a deeply psychological process that redefines the developmental trajectory of those affected, especially children. For instance, the disruption of early childhood experiences can hinder the development of basic trust, leading to difficulties in forming secure relationships later in life. Adolescents may struggle with a fractured sense of self, caught between the old world they left behind and the new world they must negotiate. The resilience displayed by these families, their ability to adapt under extreme stress, and their pursuit of stability and identity highlight the complexities of human development under duress.

4
Czechlish

Growing up bilingual and bicultural

Some masterpieces of art punch you in the gut. You instantly see your truth in their truth. Sometimes that truth is in language. In Junot Díaz's The Brief Wondrous Life of Oscar Wao (2007), a Dominican-American narrator blends English and Spanish into Spanglish:

> Lola … would eat a fat cat in front of you without a speck of vergüenza. When she was in fourth grade she'd been attacked by an older acquaintance and surviving that urikán of pain, judgment, and bochinche had made her tougher than adamantine.

Anthony Burgess's A Clockwork Orange (1962) is narrated in Nadsat, a fictional mix of English and Russian:

> There was me and my three droogs … and we sat in the Korova Milkbar making up our rassoodocks what to do with the evening … The Korova Milkbar was a milk-plus mesto …. They had no licence for selling liquor, but there was no law yet against prodding some of the new veshches which they used to put into the old moloko, so

> you could peet it with vellocet or synthemesc or dren-
> crom or one or two other veshches ...

These voices plunge me into viscerally familiar territory: straddling that borderland between two worlds, two identities. Being
both and neither. In these novels, the absence of any markers to
distinguish one language from another immerses us in this limi-
nal reality (Kingery, 2019).

> When you have two identities, you end up living in this
> limbo, caught between both places and not fully part
> of either. But it's important to see that this in-between
> space is still a real place—it's not just some nowhere
> land.
>
> —Lucia, displaced at 14 in 1967

Introduction

In this chapter, we delve into the world of Czechlish—a hybrid
language that emerges from the blending of Czech and
English—exploring how it reflects the lived experiences of individuals straddling two cultures. Through personal stories and linguistic examples, we uncover the ways in which language serves
as both a bridge and a battleground for identity. As we explore
the nuances of Czechlish, we also gain insights into the broader
refugee experience, where the struggle to preserve one's cultural heritage while adapting to a new environment creates a
dynamic, intricate reality.

British colonization and subsequent global migration to
English-speaking countries have led to the creation of over
500 "lishes"—languages that blend English with other languages

(Lambert, 2018). One example is Czechlish (Prucha, 2018), and similar ideas apply to Slovak and English.

Like other blends, Czechlish is mostly spoken, so there are no books or written works in Czechlish. A handful of sociolinguistic studies look at Czechlish from the nineteenth century to today, but it's a language that's slowly fading away (Castle, 2021). Czechlish is a hybrid language, meaning it develops among bilingual groups and mixes elements from two languages. Hybrids often develop among children raised in bilingual homes, who then continue to use the hybrid language as adults.

Czechlish applies English grammar that is uncommon in Czech, such as the subject-verb-object sentence structure and use of personal pronouns (Castle, 2021). Also, English words get Czech endings, such as when the English "shopping" and its Czech equivalent, "nakupovat," merge into "shopovat." As one participant said:

> I recently found out that I actually made up a word. Somebody joked that I should patent it. I had combined two words and was convinced I didn't invent it.
>
> —Madeleine, displaced in 1948 at 11

Another interesting feature is that Czechlish is often spoken in a childlike way. The speaker could be an actual child, but it could also be an adult who stopped learning Czech as a child. Some people in this study mentioned how their language learning was interrupted, while others talked about how different languages are tied to different stages of their lives.

My Czech is like an eight-year-old's.

—Michlean, age 8 in 1948

As many languages as you know, that's how many times you are a person.

—Dagmar, displaced at 16 in 1968

I'm a bit different in each of my languages. In Czech, I'm definitely a child. In Swedish, I'm a teenager. In French, I'm a budding young model. And in English, I'm a mom and wife.

—Paulina, displaced at age 8 in 1973

Most people in this study said their families continued speaking Czech or Slovak at home after moving to a new country. But as we can see, the actual language experience is more complicated. If a child arrived before their teenage years (Rumbaut's 1.75 and 1.5 generations), they probably grew up speaking English and Czechlish (or its Slovak equivalent).

But if they arrived during their teenage years (Rumbaut's 1.25 generation), it's likely they spoke Czech and yet another variant, Czenglish. Czenglish (or its Slovak equivalent) is an interlanguage of English words with Czech (Slovak) grammar and syntax (Sparling, Simona, & Rance, 2021). This is spoken by adult learners of English. Czech, Czechlish, and Czenglish are all distinct from each other.

When two languages collide, it's like a big crash—grammar bits fly everywhere and then get pieced back together in what some might call a linguistic junkyard. But I'm fascinated by the intuitive, logical creativity of the children inventing Czechlish.

On the other hand, some families stopped speaking Czech or Slovak altogether.

> We didn't speak Czech at home. My parents' attitude was, "You're in America now. The best thing you can do is assimilate as quickly as possible—learn the language, adapt to the culture, and move on. Stop dwelling on the past."
>
> —George D., displaced at age 4 in 1950

Another language issue people faced was how Czech or Slovak changed over generations. Since the Czechoslovak diaspora communities were isolated from their home country, their language stayed the same while the language back home evolved. This became clear to those who arrived as children as well as to those who later realized that their own Czech or Slovak had become outdated.

> When we arrived in Chicago, we walked down a windy, littered street in a Czech neighborhood. It was hot and almost empty. Passing a travel agency, we overheard people speaking old-fashioned Czech, using words like "brother" and "sister" in a peculiar accent.
>
> —Vladimir, displaced at age 16 in 1968

> As I got to know more people in the Czech Republic on return visits, I realized that some of the words I spoke were archaic.
>
> —Madeleine, displaced in 1948 at age 11

Language and power were also big issues. Many participants had seen how language could be used to oppress. The ruling group would impose their language on those they conquered. The pre-ferred response was passive resistance.

> We had to learn German, but as a point of patriotism, we made sure not to do well.
>
> —Barbara, displaced at 13 in 1948

> If you wanted to be a cool kid, you'd have As and Bs in everything except Russian, where you'd have a D as a sign of protest.
>
> —Vladimir, displaced at 16 in 1968.

My mother spent half of her 88 years in Czechoslovakia and the other half in the United States. In all that time, she never learned English. She refused. This caused tension in our family because we always had to interpret for her. I didn't understand why she was so stubborn. But now I do.

Mother had gone through both the German and the Russian indoctrinations, and her refusal to learn yet another language was her form of resistance. It was her way of defying my father, and the United States, which she blamed for giving Czechoslovakia to the Soviets at Yalta. But when a country welcomes you, like the U.S. had, it's unseemly to reject it. So, with no other outlet for her anger, she took it out on us, her family.

On a side note, Mother also refused to learn to drive. Not only was this inconvenient, but it also meant she didn't have a driver's license. For years, when asked for ID when writing a check, she would slam her old Czechoslovak passport on the counter, silently daring the bewildered cashier to deal with it. This embarrassed me to no end as a teenager.

Because Mother didn't speak English, I found it harder to talk to her as time went on. After I left home at eighteen, I experienced the "use it or lose it" phenomenon. Over the years, it became harder to fully express myself in Czech. Even though therapists encouraged me to share my feelings with my mother, it was linguistically impossible (there were no translation apps back then). The Czechoslovak cultural norm of stoicism also made it hard. As the language barrier grew, I spoke less and less to Mother in the last couple decades of her life, and mostly just listened (admittedly, this was also a function of her overbearing personality).

> Speaking to my father in English still feels unnatural, yet my Czech is fading. It's a common issue for immigrant children.
>
> —Yvette, displaced at 10 in 1968.

What's in a name?

Almost all of us had to change our names when our families moved to North America. Names were Anglicized. Spellings were changed. Diacritics disappeared. For women, the feminine endings of our family names were often changed to masculine. In Czech and Slovak, all female family names end in -á or -ová. But North American immigration officials typically changed wives' and daughters' family names to the father's name, as is customary in English.

> My passport says Lukáš, but everywhere else in the world, it's Luke. As a kid, I wanted to fit in, but now I kind of wish I had kept my original name.
>
> —Luke, displaced at age 9 in 1980

I discovered from an archived document that my last name changed from Potocká to Potocky the very day we left Prague and landed in Vienna an hour later. Ever since, I've had a feminine first name with a masculine last name, which sounds absurd in Czech or Slovak. Not to mention that a "c" before a "k" is voiced in Czech and Slovak, but is silent in English. I have three choices: succumb to the new pronunciation, change the spelling, or correct and explain—all of which I'd rather avoid.

My father, previously Pavel, became Paul. This was not Father's first effort at nominal assimilation. Before he became the Czech Pavel Potocký, he was the Jewish Ruben Auerbach. My brother, Jan, became Michael J. to stop the teasing he endured for having a female English name. As to my mother, she did not associate with "Americans" and did not change her first name.

Like my father and brother, most participants changed their first or last names to make them easier for English speakers to pronounce.

> My mom was born Vlasta, but she changed her name to Sandra when we came here because people butchered her name.
>
> —Yvette, displaced at age 10 in 1968

Some, like my mother, resented these changes to these identity markers that hold deep personal, family, cultural, and historical meaning.

> I never legally changed my name. I'm Jaroslava, not Jerri. I wish Americans weren't so insular and would make an effort to pronounce foreign names correctly. Even

people with complicated names should be able to use their real names.

Home life and ethnic communities

Just like they kept their language, most families continued to practice traditional Czech or Slovak customs at home. Participants mostly mentioned traditional foods and activities during holidays like Christmas and Easter. The same was true in my family. These stories show the different ways families navigated their new lives, communities, and identities. Some kept strong ties to their roots through community organizations, cultural activities, and social gatherings, finding comfort and connection in shared traditions. Others distanced themselves from their heritage, focusing on fitting into American society by learning English and forming relationships outside their ethnic communities. Their stories highlight the different ways these families balanced preserving their cultural identity with integrating into their new homeland.

Our family didn't assimilate well because all our friends were Czech. If I wanted to do something, it wasn't allowed because it wasn't something we did, which kept me separated from others. This feeling of being on the fringes rather than part of the crowd stayed with me through my formative years.

—Hana, displaced at age 1 in 1948

There's a Czech American club in Dallas. When we first came, they tried to get my mom involved, but she was a working mom with two teenagers, and she had a tough job. Her attitude was, "We're in America now; let's move forward."

—Yvette, displaced at age 10 in 1968

Some participants mentioned being involved in "Falcon", a Czechoslovak nationalistic gymnastics movement brought over by earlier immigrants, which provided a strong ethnic community.

My parents weren't involved in the Czech community, and they wanted us to speak English so they could learn it better, but we rebelled. I quickly became part of the Czech community because I met my future Czech husband in high school. We had balls and the Sokol Hall. The Czech community was fairly big.

—Dagmar, displaced at age 16 in 1968

We moved to 71st Street in New York and lived across from Sokol Hall. I got really involved there, starting at age six. I went to Sokol camp in Connecticut and spent a few summers there, getting out of the heat of the city.

—Pavel, displaced at age 1 in 1949

Economic struggles

Many participants recalled how their parents made big sacrifices and worked hard after moving to the new country. Their parents often worked in tough, low-paying jobs like domestic servants, factory workers, and clerks, even if they had higher education. They faced language barriers, cultural isolation, and exploitation at work. In return, we, their children, often felt a strong sense of responsibility not to disappoint them.

My parents worked as domestic servants. They worked hard, saved, and didn't take any vacations. They did it mostly for the children. We never had the typical rebellious teenage years because I saw how hard my parents worked. I couldn't imagine talking back to them or doing anything like that.

—Duke, displaced at 8 in 1948

My father started as a supermarket laborer, coming home exhausted, and later worked as a Wall Street clerk while giving piano lessons at night. My mother spent over 20 years on an assembly line. I felt a deep responsibility to succeed, knowing these opportunities wouldn't exist in Czechoslovakia, carrying the weight of my family's sacrifices even as a young teen.

—Susan, displaced at 14 in 1969

For some, this sense of duty became a lifelong legacy, a desire to honor their parents' sacrifices by succeeding and helping others.

I'm old. My father's dead. And I'm still the perfect daughter.

—Madeleine, displaced at 11 in 1948

These stories also touch on the emotional toll these hardships took on our families, especially on our parents, who had to adjust to a new and often unwelcoming environment.

My parents tried to do what they thought was best by learning the language, but that took something away from us. The adaptation process was much harder for them. My mom had a particularly tough time because she lost her friends and family. She went from work-ing a hospital job to pressing laundry at a laundromat. She cried a lot, which she never did before we left Czechoslovakia. My dad struggled to find a good job that paid him what he was worth. People often took advantage of him, thinking he didn't deserve fair pay because he was an immigrant.

—Petra, displaced at 7 in 1986

Parentification

Sometimes, the child's sense of responsibility developed very early, flipping the parent-child roles. This process, known as par-entification, has been noted in immigrant and refugee families (Weisskirch, 2010).

A few days after we arrived in New York, I wanted to enroll in school. I didn't know schools were called public schools, so I looked for "schools" in the phone book and found secretarial schools. Eventually, I asked a doorman who pointed me to a high school. I registered myself but had to ask my father to come with me to complete the process.

—Susan, displaced at 14 in 1969

My parents promptly divorced within the first three weeks after my arrival in Sweden. My brother and I were left to fend for ourselves, and I took care of us. Christmas was sad because it was just my mother, my little brother, and me, and my mother was working. I tried to give my little brother as much of a Christmas as I could by making my own Mikuláš uniform and playing the role when I was 10.

—Paulina, displaced at 8 in 1973

Initial adjustment to environment and school

For some, the sudden change in climate was a shock that required adjustment.

> New York City was hot, humid, and smelly in July. We weren't prepared for it, coming from a cooler European summer. We had no real idea what to expect in the United States.
>
> —Susan, displaced at age 14 in 1969

> I really disliked Los Angeles because of the weather. It was arid and desert-like, and I missed the greenery and nature of Slovakia.
>
> —Lucia, displaced at age 14 in 1967

For many of us, the early weeks, months, or years in the new country were filled with isolation and cultural dislocation. Some of us were bullied, alienated, and felt like we didn't belong.

> High school was pretty horrible. My mom would dress me differently than all the other American kids, and I had a language disadvantage. They could tell I was different.
>
> —Peter, displaced at 7 in 1980

> The other kids made fun of me because they thought we came from some kind of backwater.
>
> —George G., displaced at age 15 in 1968

Some of us internalized the negative messages we heard.

> As a child, I wasn't interested in Czechoslovakia. It felt closed off, with little news reaching us, and it seemed as bleak as any other Eastern European country. I was almost ashamed of being Czech. In the 1970s, *Saturday Night Live* even had a skit with Dan Aykroyd and Steve Martin as goofy Czechs, which reinforced the stereotype. So I rarely mentioned my Czech heritage.
>
> —Duke, displaced at age 8 in 1948

Others, however, didn't have trouble in school.

> In high school I was one of the rock 'n' roll kids, so I had a lot of good friends and good memories.
>
> —Petra, displaced at 7 in 1986

> In high school, the older kids were nice to me. They liked that I was learning English, and it was kind of cool. Most of my friends were American.
>
> —Alex, displaced at 17 in 1983

When we first enrolled in school, many of us who had previous schooling in Czechoslovakia found that we were ahead of our classmates in our new country. I went to first grade in Czechoslovakia and started second grade in New York the next year. While I already knew cursive writing, my classmates were just learning to print. And while I knew fractions, my classmates were learning addition.

> In Czechoslovakia, I had a lot more subjects than here, and it didn't seem as tough.
>
> —Vaclav, displaced at 13 in 1969

By the time I came to eighth grade, I'd already had phys-ics, chemistry, and math. I was like two years ahead of what we were covering in earth science here.

—Paul, displaced at age 14 in 1968

Overall, we did well academically, but navigating the educational system and extracurricular activities was sometimes challenging.

I adjusted quickly and didn't have problems in school. But I stopped doing extracurricular activities. My parents worked day and night, and our life got smaller once we moved here because they didn't know the system. My life became home-based.

—Yvette, displaced at 10 in 1968.

I was never advised on college applications. In Czechoslovakia, you applied after graduation, so we assumed the same here. With my art teacher's help, I prepared a portfolio and got into art school.

—Lucia, displaced at 14 in 1967

We had a lot of adjusting to do, especially in school and social interactions. It was a challenge we had to over-come to understand how things worked outside our immediate environment.

—Luke, displaced at 9 in 1980

Summary and conclusions

As reflected in these narratives, the journey of growing up bilin-gual and bicultural reveals the complex interplay between lan-guage, identity, and culture. As we've seen, Czechlish is more than just a linguistic blend; it's a manifestation of the lived reality of straddling two worlds. The stories in this chapter illustrate the challenges and triumphs of maintaining one's cultural heritage while navigating a new cultural landscape. Whether through the creative use of language, the preservation of traditions, or the adaptation to new social environments, these experiences highlight the resilience and adaptability of those who live in the space between two identities. Czechlish, in all its forms, serves as a reminder that language is not just a tool for communication, but a living, evolving reflection of our identities and histories.

5
Inherited shadows
Historical trauma

Growing up, I always knew that my father's parents had been murdered in the concentration camps. However, I don't remember anyone actually telling me this. It was just something I knew, as if it was absorbed from the atmosphere around me. Over time, as I dug into letters from surviving relatives, connected with strangers across the globe, and did my own research, I started piecing together the story.

Introduction

History doesn't just stay in the past—it sticks with us, shaping who we are and how we see the world. This chapter dives into how the traumatic experiences of one generation can ripple through time, affecting the lives of their descendants in ways that are often subtle but powerful.

This is, in part, a personal exploration of how the Holocaust left its mark on my own family, silently shaping my identity and understanding of the world. The unspoken stories from my parents, the bits and pieces of history I uncovered—they all hung over my childhood like a shadow. My father's family, who perished in

Figure 3 Multigenerational childhood forced migration: The author's father (back row, left) and uncle (second row, second from right) among other Czech Jewish refugee children and their foster mother, Penkhull Children's Home, Stoke-on-Trent, England, 1939.

the camps, and my mother's life of displacement and loss, were always there, even when they weren't directly talked about. These untold stories, passed down through silence and subtle hints, have deeply influenced my life and those of others who carry the burden of a history we didn't live but can't escape.

This chapter is about how trauma is passed down through generations. Through personal stories, historical facts, and the experiences of others who share similar legacies, we'll look at how the Holocaust shaped the identities of survivors and their descendants. We'll explore how these deep-seated traumas continue to shape who we are and how we view the world today.

My father

My father's parents met in Prague in 1920. They were Zionists; in 1922, they moved to Palestine (today Israel) and helped establish Kibbutz Bet Alpha, which still exists. My father was born there on New Year's Eve in 1924, and his brother, my uncle, came four years later. They lived on the kibbutz until 1931, when they moved back to Prague.

At the same time, Hitler was rising to power. By 1939, my father's parents saw the peril to Jews. That year, a British man named Nicholas Winton organized transports to get Jewish children out of Czechoslovakia. He, his mother, and a few friends ultimately saved 669 Czechoslovak Jewish children—a story that's been told in books and movies.

The British authorities required each child to have a sponsor in England who would promise to take care of them. Family friends from the kibbutz days had already fled Prague for England. They lived in Stoke-on-Trent, a city in central England. They convinced the city council to open an empty orphanage to serve as a group home for my father, his brother, and six other Czech Jewish refugee kids. Thus my father and his brother became two of Nicholas Winton's 669 rescued children.

After journeying from Prague to the Netherlands by train and from there ship carried them across the English Channel, my father spent his teenage years in that group home. When he turned 18, he joined the Czechoslovak Independent Brigade in Great Britain, which served at Dunkirk. After the war, he returned to Prague to find out what had happened to his parents. He went to their old apartment, finding it empty.

Five members of my father's family were murdered in the Holocaust: his mother, father, paternal grandmother, and two uncles. Five others survived the concentration camps and death marches: his maternal grandmother, three aunts, and a first cousin.

After the war, my father lived with an army buddy and attended technical school. He joined the Communist Party, viewing it as part of his parents' social idealist legacy. He was initially considered a promising Party member. Later, however, Party purges targeted Party members who had served with Western Allies during the war and Jews. Being both, my father was advised to "get to know the working class better," and sent to work as a coal miner for several years. He later returned to Prague, working as a locksmith and mechanic. Disillusioned by the 1956 Soviet invasion of Hungary, he left the Party, facing considerable pressure to remain (Centropa, 2023).

The 1968 Soviet-led invasion was the last straw for my father. He felt he had to leave. He spent several months contacting distant family friends from the kibbutz who then lived in New York City. They agreed to sponsor our family. He also badgered my mother, who did not want to leave her own aging mother. Finally, he obtained government permission for the family to fly to Vienna on a tourist visa. Once there, he applied for asylum.

My mother

My mother was born in 1925 into a Catholic family in the part of Czechoslovakia known as Sudety (Sudetenland in German), on the German border. Her father was the principal of a girls' school, and the family lived in a large apartment in the school building. In 1938, when Mother was 13, Czechoslovakia's allies, Britain and France, betrayed the country by letting Hitler annex the Sudetenland without consulting Czechoslovakia. When the Nazis took over the territory, the Czechs living there, including Mother's family, were expelled.

The family was internally displaced to Prague, where they lived through the war. Living through the war meant starvation, icicles hanging from the bedroom ceiling in the winters, tuberculosis, no menstrual products, and the daily humiliation of life under occupation.

Thirty years later, when Mother was 43, she had to leave her home again after my father decided we should emigrate following the Soviet invasion. This final move was one she never got over.

Mother wasn't what we call "resilient" today. She never accepted the loss of her homeland or the people she left behind. For the rest of her life, she lived in a world of letters, corresponding with friends and family back in Czechoslovakia, lost in the memories of her childhood, before the Nazis and Communists took over.

At every family meal, she would reminisce about her idyllic, pre-Nazi childhood in her small village, where everyone knew everyone. She would recite the names of all her classmates—people I had never met and never would. She'd talk about what these people were doing now—who was sick, who had ungrateful kids, who needed something sent. She generally skipped over the war years and picked the story back up in the 1950s, when she was in her twenties. She would recount trips and hikes across Czechoslovakia with some guy. Over time, I tuned out these compulsive recitations. I never thought about who this guy in my mother's life was, but as a teen I found old papers and realized he was her ex-husband. Only years later did it strike me how strange it was for a woman to constantly reminisce about her ex in front of her second husband and their children.

Others' mothers and fathers

As described earlier, a handful of the 1948 group had first-hand memories of the Second World War, but these childhood memories were fleeting. However, 9 of the 18 participants in the 1948 group, as well as one member of the 1968 group, shared detailed stories of their parents' Holocaust persecution.

Their narratives give us a glimpse into the lives of families deeply shaped by the Holocaust. These stories of the second generation reveal the intersections of identity, the lasting impact of trauma, and the profound loss experienced by those who lived through one of the darkest periods in human history. From the discovery of hidden Jewish heritage to the lifelong burden of survivor's guilt, each story highlights the unique and often painful ways the Holocaust continues to echo through generations. Through these narratives, we gain a better understanding of the Holocaust's lasting impact on individuals, families, and communities, as well as the ongoing struggle to come to terms with a history that is both intensely personal and universally significant.

Discovery and identity

Some participants suddenly and shockingly discovered their Jewish heritage and the reality of their families' Holocaust experiences, which completely changed how they saw themselves and their family histories.

> I was raised a Catholic and married an Episcopalian. Then I found out I was Jewish. That was very difficult. In 1996, I got a letter with accurate details saying the writer knew my family and they were a Jewish family. I was stunned. It's one thing to find out you're Jewish. It's another that people had been sent to concentration camps.
>
> —Madeleine, displaced at 11 in 1948

> I didn't know that all of these things happened to me and my family because I was actually three-quarters Jewish even though I was brought up Catholic.
>
> —Charles, displaced at 12 1948

Intergenerational trauma and the legacy of silence

"I set out to find a group of people who, like me, were possessed by a history they had never lived." When I read these words by Helen Epstein over forty years ago, they changed my life. Suddenly, I understood my dysfunctional family and realized that I wanted to help others with similar experiences.

Helen was born in Prague in 1947 to Holocaust survivor parents. Her family moved to New York a year later. Her 1979 book, Children of the Holocaust, explored the trauma passed down from Holocaust survivors to their children. Through personal stories, interviews, and psychological insights, she showed how the trauma of the Holocaust was handed down to the next generation.

Her book looked into the psychological, emotional, and social challenges faced by these children, who often grew up in homes marked by silence, fear, and a deep sense of loss. Helen touched on themes like a profound sense of responsibility to their parents, a struggle with identity, and a deep-seated anxiety about the future. The young adults she described often felt intense pressure to succeed, coupled with guilt and confusion about their parents' suffering. Many also had trouble forming their own relationships and wrestled with an inherited sense of vulnerability and insecurity. Helen's work on how culture, resilience, and trauma are passed from one generation to another was groundbreaking, laying the foundation for the many books and research studies that followed.

These themes are clearly reflected in the narratives of study participants.

> My grandfather, grandmother, uncle, aunt, and a cousin
> were all deported and perished in the Holocaust, a loss
> that was always in the background. My father, who

learned of his parents' fate at 23, was never truly happy afterward, likely carrying guilt for leaving on his honeymoon. Certain times of the year, especially spring—the season he knew they were taken—seemed to trouble him most.

—Michlean, displaced at 8 in 1948

We lost 15 family members; only we survived. My parents never spoke about it, hoping to shield me from trauma. But I struggled with nightmares and bedwetting due to the trauma. My parents didn't know, and I never discussed it with them.

—Charles, displaced at 12 1948

Thomas Hasler's father, Karel Hašler, was a popular Czech songwriter, actor, director, and playwright who, was arrested by the Gestapo because of the patriotic nature of his songs. He was murdered at Mauthausen concentration camp one month after Tom was born.

My mother said we left Czechoslovakia due to fear of nuclear war, but I didn't believe her, thinking she was hiding something. Later, I realized that people who endured WWII and other hardships often repress memories to find normalcy. My mother said they were too painful to remember, which I now understand.

—Thomas, displaced at 8 in 1949

Survival and guilt

Participants described the moral dilemmas and profound guilt associated with survival during the Holocaust. Their parents had to make harrowing decisions, leaving survivors with deep, unresolved guilt.

> When the war began in 1939, my father, then 18, was drafted into a special Slovak army regiment for Jews and sent to forced labor. He escaped in 1941, hid in the mountains, and joined the partisans for the last six months of the war. He rarely spoke about it. He flinched at loud noises and hated toy guns. My mother and her sister were sent to Auschwitz in June 1942. Her sister perished there, and my mom, who survived, still carries guilt, haunted by memories of her sister's death. She struggles to understand why she lived while her sister, whom she viewed as stronger and better, did not.
>
> —George G., displaced at 15 in 1968

While most survivors didn't talk much about their experiences, some couldn't stop. Jerri Zbiral was born a few years after the war. Her mother survived the Lidice atrocity. This Czech village was demolished by Nazi troops in 1942 in retaliation for the Czechoslovaks' assassination of Hitler's commander in Prague. The village's women were separated from their children and sent to concentration camps, while all the men were taken to a farm and shot. The Nazis burned the town to the ground and vowed to obliterate its name from the map of Europe (U.S. Holocaust Memorial Museum, 2021).

Jerri's mother and grandmother spent the last three years of the war in a concentration camp, while Jerri's older sister was sent to live in Germany as part of the Nazi Lebensborn program. Jerri's mother walked back to Czechoslovakia after the war and reunited with her daughter, Jerri's older sister. She later married Jerri's father and had Jerri.

> Over and over again, every day, there was something that triggered my mother to tell me what happened in the concentration camp. Towards the end of the war, my grandmother was selected for transport to Auschwitz, from which no one returned. She panicked and insisted my mother accompany her. My mother bribed a guard to join the transport, then she bribed another guard to get them off, replacing them with two others who were sent to their deaths. This decision haunted me. But my mother saw it as necessary for survival. You think, what would you do in that situation?
>
> —Jerri Z., displaced at 1 in 1949

Impact of loss and the burden of history

The survivors' children mourned the family members they never knew and bore the heavy burden of their historical legacy.

> The fact that I never got to meet my grandparents and other relatives is very painful. It's one thing if a person is taken because they're ill. But it's even worse knowing that they died such horrible deaths. With my uncle and aunt and cousin, I really don't know exactly what happened. They could have been used for forced labor and might have lived for three or four years. Who knows what awful life they might have had?
>
> —Michlean, displaced at 8 in 1948

I believe it's incumbent on all of us, especially someone like me, who is a direct child of survivors, to say: Look, first of all, it happened. This was the largest mass murder in history. Second of all, it's still happening now in various forms.

—George G., displaced at 15 in 1968

Communist trauma?

When I started writing this chapter, I expected to find that people from the 1968 wave and later would talk about the historical trauma of living under Communist totalitarian oppression. After all, their families had been under Communist rule for twenty years. In my mind, the Holocaust and Communism blended together into one big evil.

But to my surprise, this group barely mentioned historical trauma. Only a few talked about the Second World War, and just a handful mentioned the injustices their parents faced under Communism. They didn't discuss psychological impacts of communism on themselves, except for how it shaped their political opinions.

Summary and conclusions

Reflecting on the stories and insights shared in this chapter, it becomes clear that the experiences of those who lived through the Holocaust left deep, lasting scars that continue to resonate across generations. The trauma of such an event is not just a personal burden but an intergenerational one, shaping the identities and worldviews of the descendants in profound ways.

The stories in this chapter show how the unresolved traumas of the previous generation can complicate childhood development as the children of survivors often struggle to reconcile their inherited histories with their emerging identities. The sense of guilt, loss, and the heavy burden of the past can create confusion about who they are and where they belong, leading to an identity that is both deeply connected to and conflicted by history.

Later in life, as we review our life journey, we seek a sense of fulfillment and purpose. For many whose families lived through the Holocaust, this life stage involves not only personal reflection but also an attempt to make sense of the suffering endured by their families and their communities.

Ultimately, this chapter highlights how the type of trauma experienced—whether total war like the Second World War or cold war persecution like Communist oppression—can have different intergenerational impacts. While both are undeniably traumatic, the stories here suggest that the immediacy and brutality of the Holocaust created a more deeply embedded psychological legacy than the more prolonged but less overtly violent experience of living under Communist rule.

While each generation faces its own developmental challenges, those living in the shadow of immense historical trauma have an added burden. Our journey through life is intertwined with the unresolved crises of our ancestors.

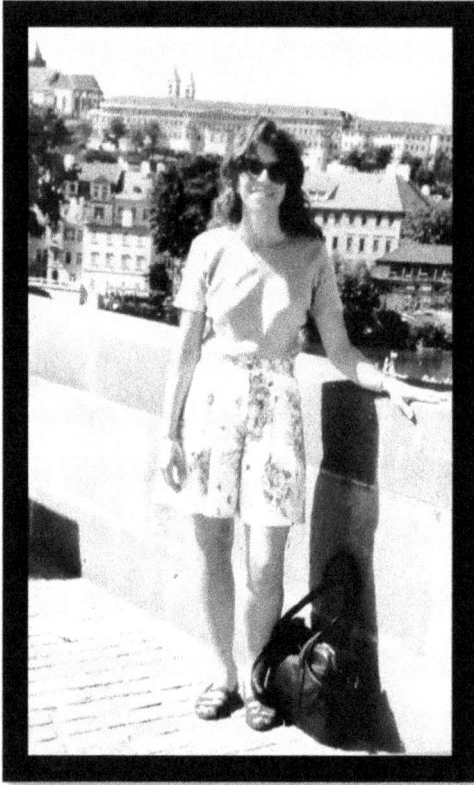

Figure 4 Returned Czech, Prague, 1995.

6
Returned Czechs

Retracing roots

In the summer of 1995, I returned to my homeland. It was a journey in search of identity. I followed tracks that had been laid before I was born. I experienced an adrenaline-fueled hyperawareness. All my sensations were heightened, as though my mind and body wanted to absorb in a few weeks what I had missed for 26 years.

I walked for miles throughout the city, feeling every pebble, every cobblestone, every marble church floor. I searched for familiar sights—a street corner, a stairway, a building—fleeting images that had passed through my mind for a quarter century. They were the thin threads that connected me to my birthplace. It was as though I needed to prove to myself that those places I imagined really did exist.

Mostly, I didn't see familiar sights. But at the same time, nothing was unfamiliar. I had viewed so many photos of Prague over the years. When I occasionally found that familiar street corner, stairway, or building, I felt electrified. Prague and I were no longer bound by a thin thread—there was a live current between us.

I heard every scrap of conversation uttered by passing strangers. I marveled at the peculiar inflection of their speech. Although I understood the words, the tone was foreign to me. Relatives told me I have an American accent, lacking the singsong lilt of Prague Czech. Thereafter, I listened even more intently to that lilt and tried to mimic it, but I don't think I succeeded.

I savored the unique scent of Czech beer pubs—something I remembered from childhood and hadn't found in the U.S. I felt as though I needed to build up a store of sensory memories to carry with me upon my return to the States. I tried to absorb the essence of Czech culture. I went to concerts, chamber recitals, operas, art galleries, museums, cathedrals, synagogues, castles, and monuments—trying to grasp the cultural heritage I was born into.

Nowhere were my senses more alert than in the Prague metro. Standing in a crowded train, feeling the forces of acceleration and deceleration swaying me back and forth, enveloped by darkness, I stared at the faces of my fellow passengers, searching for commonalities, trying to discern the Czechs from the tourists.

I scrutinized the passengers' attire. I peered over shoulders to read newspapers, marveling that they could read Czech so casually. I looked so intently at the advertisements lining the train walls that, by the end of my two-week stay, I practically had them memorized. At each stop, I listened to the robotic voice announcing, "Complete your embarkation and debarkation. The doors are closing." I got tireless pleasure from hearing the perfect Czech enunciation with which these pronouncements were made.

Underlying all my intense scrutiny of faces, hands, clothing, and shoes, was the knowledge that I was born to be one of them—that it should have been me sitting so casually on that train, seemingly oblivious to all the symbols and meanings it held. Instead, history had made me an observer—a witness to my own possible other life.

Introduction

All of the children in this study ultimately made the pilgrimage to the land of our birth once we were adults. As we journeyed back to our birthplace decades later, we encountered a blend of nostalgia, reconnection, and the stark realities of change. These return visits reaffirmed our roots and brought a sense of closure, while also highlighting the distance that time created between our past and present selves. These narratives reveal the intricate dance between heritage and identity, the challenges of passing on cultural traditions, the lingering effects of trauma, and the gratitude mixed with regret that shape our reflections on life. The following accounts delve into these themes, offering a window into the experiences of those who have lived with the duality of belonging to two worlds.

Return journeys

Returning to our birthplace after years away, we encountered a place both familiar and transformed. The return was a profound and emotional reconnection with our roots, a reminder of where we came from and what we had lost. At the same time, the visit often stirred up feelings of alienation and disappointment. The contrast between past and present, and the struggle to reconcile personal and cultural identities, added further layers to the emotional landscape of these return visits.

> Returning to Prague for the first time was deeply emotional. The city's beauty and history captivated me, and I felt a strong connection to my roots, especially after my mother's passing just before Communism fell. I felt a need to experience what she had missed.
>
> —Ivana, displaced 3 in 1949

> My mother and I went back to Czechoslovakia for the first time in the late '90s, after being away for decades. It was surreal. The memories flooded back, and it was like walking through a dream. Everything was the same, yet different, and it stirred up all sorts of emotions.
>
> —Yvette, displaced at 10 in 1968.

> Going back to the Czech Republic after college was magical. The castles, the cobblestone streets, the stained glass in the cathedrals—it all felt like stepping into a fairytale.
>
> —Luke, displaced at 9 in 1980

Most of us were not able to visit Czechoslovakia until the Cold War ended in 1989 because we were considered criminals by the Czechoslovak government for leaving and would have been arrested. Some, however, were able to visit during the Cold War era. They uniformly used the word "grey" to describe the country. Other adjectives included bleak, lifeless, dreary, dirty, miserable, filthy, neglected, depressing, and hopeless.

In the 1970s, I flew to Frankfurt, rented a car, and drove to the border. When I got there, I found a radio station playing songs I knew, which made me emotional. I started crying as I drove. During that visit, the atmosphere was bleak—no music, no life. Seeing people trudging around confirmed my expectations.

—Duke, displaced at 8 in 1948

Visiting Czechoslovakia in 1968 was strange. I had grown up speaking Czech at home, but being fully immersed in it was something else. The city was dreary, gray, and dirty, with people visibly miserable. Yet, hearing everyone speak Czech in public spaces was oddly comforting, almost like a genetic memory.

—Jerri, displaced at 1 in 1949

Returning was a disorienting experience, especially when familiar faces from the past emerged from the haze of forgotten memories. Reconnecting with childhood friends could bring either disappointment or joy.

In 1991, we took a trip back to Slovakia. It was strange because I had forgotten almost everyone. Meeting a friend I hadn't seen in 12 years was shocking—he remembered me, but I struggled to recall him at first, which bothered me. We reconnected but didn't maintain those friendships.

—Paul, displaced at 14 in 1968

In 1994, after the Velvet Revolution, Prague had changed dramatically. I met my best childhood friend in Prague after 29 years without contact. We reconnected, and it felt like no time had passed, as if we were soulmates, despite our very different lives. I also reconnected with my old schoolmates, and our bond remained strong.

—Susan, displaced at 14 in 1969

Returning to familiar places after years away can evoke a powerful mix of emotions, where past and present collide. For many, the journey back to our childhood neighborhood was an intense emotional awakening, as if reabsorbing memories long forgotten. Others struggled to reconcile different aspects of their identity during their visit, finding that the expectations of others overshadowed the personal connection they sought, leaving them conflicted about returning.

Memories flooded in. It was like comparing the past with the present. Walking through the old neighborhoods, everything looked the same except for the cars and billboards. It was an emotional rollercoaster. I felt like a dried-up sponge soaking in water, expanding emotionally. It was as if I had been asleep and was suddenly waking up.

—Yvette, displaced at 10 in 1968.

When I returned in 1991, it was difficult to reconcile my different perspectives—American, Czech, child, and adult. I wanted to reconnect with my childhood self—Pavlínka. But people there saw me as the famous model Paulina Porizkova, which took away the enjoyment. I didn't stay long and didn't want to return often. Although I feel a deep connection to the place, like an umbilical cord, I don't feel the need to go back frequently.

—Paulina, displaced at 8 in 1973

Navigating bicultural identity

The complex interaction of heritage and identity was a common thread among participants. All claimed a bicultural identity that fully embraced their new lives, while continuing to cherish and maintain their cultural roots. From celebrating holidays in traditional ways to feeling a deep yet sometimes conflicted connection to their homeland, we embodied this duality.

> I've always felt like I'm neither fully Czech nor fully American—somewhere in between. That's kept me on the fringe, but it's also given me a broader perspective. I'm too American to be European and too European to be 100% American, but I've learned to embrace that.
>
> —Hana, displaced at 1 in 1948

> I feel more American because I've spent most of my life here, but deep down, I'm still Slovak. For now, we keep our traditions alive, especially at Christmas. It's my way of staying connected to the place I still think of as home.
>
> —Petra, displaced at 7 in 1986

> Once you leave where you grew up, you can never truly go back—it's not the same, and you're not fully part of the new place either. But I'm content. I keep our Slovak traditions alive in my home. I feel more Slovak than American, which varies depending on life stages. Right

now, I'm more Slovak, mainly because my children are interested in it.

—Lucia, displaced at 14 in 1967

When I return, I'm a foreigner. Having lived in the U.S. most of my life, I'm more of a Czech-American than an American. In Prague, people don't see me as Czech. We still keep traditions. That first trip back opened my eyes and made me rethink my identity. I began exploring aspects of my heritage, realizing they were part of who I am.

—Yvette, displaced at 10 in 1968

Prague Spring and Soviet invasion

Those whose families fled Czechoslovakia before 1968 witnessed the Prague Spring and Soviet-led invasion from afar. For some, the Prague Spring rekindled a sense of identity and a connection to their roots. For others, it was a time of hope tempered by skepticism, knowing that the newly granted freedoms might not last. The invasion that followed left a lasting impact, evoking strong emotions and a sense of loss among those who watched the events unfold from afar.

I didn't pay much attention until 1968, when the Prague Spring happened. It felt like a different world, and suddenly, I felt connected to my Czech roots. I started listening to Radio Prague on my shortwave radio. Hearing Czech again made me feel both American and Czech. But after the invasion I put the curtain down again. I really didn't care.

—Charles, displaced at 12 in 1948

I vividly remember watching the news about the invasion with my mother in Montréal. We were both in tears.

—Jerri, displaced at 1 in 1949

Velvet revolution

In November 1989, the Velvet Revolution swept Czechoslovakia— seven days of peaceful mass demonstrations that resulted in the collapse of the Communist regime that had gripped the nation for 41 years. As I watched the demonstrations on the nightly news from half a world away, I was stunned, not knowing what to feel. I felt elation. I felt reborn along with Czechoslovakia. But I also felt a twinge of loneliness. I wanted celebrate with fellow Czechoslovaks.

The Velvet Revolution of 1989 was a pivotal moment that deeply resonated with all of us, each experiencing a wave of emotions as we watched history unfold from afar. For most of us, it was an unexpected and surreal event, once again rekindling a deep connection to our roots and stirring memories of our past. We felt a renewed sense of identity, while also grappling with the challenges of reconciling our distant lives with the dramatic changes in our native land.

The Velvet Revolution changed everything. I remember watching it unfold, feeling this incredible connection to my Czech roots.

—Charles, displaced at 12 in 1948

The 1989 revolution was significant to me. I felt isolated living in Iceland, not speaking the language and without the internet, wishing I could be there and do something. It was a huge moment for me.

—George G., displaced at 15 in 1968

I followed the fall of Communism in 1989 but I felt dis-connected. It was hard to fully grasp that after decades, Communism had suddenly ended.

—Yvette, displaced at 10 in 1968.

After the Velvet Revolution, many of us considered returning to Czechoslovakia to live. Ultimately, however, none of us did. Over time, the lives we had built—family, friends, and work—often outweighed the pull of our birthplace. For many, limited Czech or Slovak proficiency was an obstacle.

I've thought about moving back, but I'm not sure how my husband would adapt.

—Petra, displaced at 7 in 1986

If I moved to Slovakia and had to work there, especially in a job that required reading and writing in Slovak, it would be a challenge.

—Paul, displaced at 14 in 1968

During our middle adulthood, some of us returned to Czechoslovakia for a few years, while others became transna-tional, making frequent trips back and forth. However, these frequent visits abated in older age as social ties to the native country diminished.

Now most of my family is gone, and I don't know many people there anymore. It would be difficult to re-estab-lish myself at this stage of life. I think I'm better off stay-ing in New York and visiting often. As you get older, you start to wonder where to spend the rest of your life, and that can be a tough decision.

—Ivana, displaced 3 in 1949

I had an apartment in Prague until four years ago, where I kept my furniture and celebrated the holidays. I would visit often, but eventually, I closed it up and brought everything back here.

—Dagmar, displaced at 16 in 1968

Return journeys in older adulthood are often as observers rather than participants.

When I'm in Prague, I like to soak up the atmosphere, sitting in a coffee house and watching the city go by. I don't tell people I'm there because my friends would fight over me for meals, wanting to talk about their lives, not realizing I'm 40 years removed from it all. I'm more of a tourist who speaks Czech. I love the city and enjoy sitting in a café, reading the newspaper, and watching the world go by. Prague is the best city in the world for that.

—George G., displaced at 15 in 1968

Preserving heritage

All of the participants valued passing on our cultural heritage to our children. All shared their traditions, language, and cultural roots with their children, seeing it as a vital connection to their past.

When my kids were born, I realized I was proud to pass on our heritage.

—Jerry, displaced at 3 in 1948.

After the borders opened, I took my kids back to show them where I came from.

—Paul, displaced at 14 in 1968

However, the pressures of daily life, coupled with some children's disinterest or struggles, often led to a gradual fading of those efforts. Despite these challenges, many maintained hope that their children would appreciate and embrace the duality of their heritage, keeping the connection alive for future generations.

> My mother tried to teach my children Czech by speaking it to them when they were little, but they got frustrated because they didn't understand. This made them lose interest in learning the language, and it eventually slipped away.
>
> —Paulina, displaced at 8 in 1973

> I tried to pass on the Czech culture to my children, telling them they were 100% Czech, sending them to Czech schools, and trying to speak the language. But like me at their age, they rebelled, and we didn't end up speaking Czech at home.
>
> —Pavel, displaced at 1 in 1949.

Confronting trauma and finding peace

For some of us, the emotional scars of the past, especially those tied to family trauma, left lasting impacts on our mental well-being. Whether grappling with the inherited pain from parents who survived horrors we can't fathom, or struggling with the sadness and disruption caused by our forced migration, many of us have had to confront deep-seated emotions to find peace. Through therapy, creative expression, and personal reflection, we have navigated our way through anger, anxiety, and a fundamental sense of loss, ultimately seeking to understand, for-give, and heal.

History leaves us with consequences we must live with, even if we weren't directly involved. I found myself angry with my mother for the ways she damaged me, though I knew she didn't intend to. She was deeply wounded her-self. Through therapy and creative work, I came to terms with my anger and accepted that, despite everything, I still loved her. Understanding her trauma, especially from her upbringing and experiences in the concentra-tion camp, helped me find peace.

—Jerri, displaced at 1 in 1949

It took me many years to come to terms with my feel-ings and forgive my parents because I always felt like I was kidnapped, being so young. Eventually, I worked through my issues with them and my childhood. I even wrote them a letter, expressing my admiration for what they did and acknowledging how difficult it must have been to raise someone like me.

—Dagmar, displaced at 16 in 1968

As a musician, there's always some level of darkness or sensitivity. Forced migration has deeply influenced this. It shaped me, leaving a fundamental sadness. Even though I enjoy life and humor, it never really goes away. When I write, it stems from the disruption of my life at age 15. Even playing a couple of polkas can touch an emotional nerve.

—George G., displaced at 15 in 1968

I've lived with anxiety since I was a small child, which can be crippling and make everyday life difficult. Sometimes it transfers into claustrophobia and agoraphobia and all sorts of little phobias. It's something that I've lived with my whole life and I'm adept at dealing with it. I think my disrupted childhood has everything to do with it. There's also a genetic predisposition. I'm writing about it and I'm in therapy.

—Paulina, displaced at 8 in 1973

Gratitudes and regrets

Older adulthood is about reflecting on our lives. Acceptance brings a sense of closure and completeness; regret leads to bitterness and despair. The participants in this study expressed both. They felt deep gratitude for the opportunities found in their new land, coupled with a deep appreciation for the sacrifices made by our parents who paved the way. For many, this gratitude grows over time, as we reflect on the courage and strength our parents exhibited in leaving everything behind to start anew.

What an absolute wonderful land of opportunity. My parents spoke no English. They escaped without much. I had all the advantages because of them.

—Duke, displaced at 8 in 1948

It was incredibly kind and brave of my mother to bring us here, leaving behind everything familiar for a new life with a different language, culture, and work. She sacrificed comfort, friends, and familiarity for our future.

> I'm grateful for the opportunities in the U.S. and for my mom's courage in making it possible.
>
> —Luke, displaced at 9 in 1980

Alongside this thankfulness, there is also regret—for not preserving the language and traditions of our heritage, for missed opportunities to connect more deeply with our parents, and for the moments that slipped away.

> If I had to do it all over, I would probably try to teach my kids the Czech language. I didn't even try because I figured the Iron Curtain would be there forever and there was no need for them to learn the language.
>
> —Paul, displaced at 14 in 1968

> My mother died prematurely in a car accident. So I never had a chance to follow up with her. I really regret that. People always tell you to record with your relatives. I should really do something like this with my own family members.
>
> —Ivana, displaced 3 in 1949

Summary and conclusions

In reflecting on these deeply personal narratives of return, it becomes evident that the journey back to one's homeland is not merely a physical voyage but an exploration of identity, belonging, and unresolved emotions. As we navigate between our heritage and the lives we have built, we grapple with the duality of being both rooted in our past and shaped by the present.

Many of us sought to reconnect with our origins, pass on cultural traditions to our children, and make sense of our bicultural identities. Whether through reconnecting with long-lost friends, revisiting childhood homes, or passing on traditions to the next generation, we sought to leave a legacy that honors the past while adapting to the future. As we move into later life, these return journeys take on an even deeper significance. This stage is characterized by reflection on our lives, where we seek to find a sense of closure and completeness. Revisiting our homeland often brings an acceptance of our life's journey, with all its complexities and contradictions. Yet the visits also stir feelings of regret, highlighting missed opportunities and the erosion of cultural ties over time.

Ultimately, these stories underscore the universal human need to reconcile the past with the present, to find peace with the choices made and the paths taken. In these journeys, we see the ongoing struggle to embrace a life lived between two worlds, finding meaning in the tension between what was left behind and what has been gained.

7
Am I still a refugee?
The lifelong journey

My husband and I recently attended an Oktoberfest celebration in our U.S. neighborhood. Oktoberfest is a traditional Bavarian beer and food festival. Because the Czech Republic's entire western border is shared with Bavaria, a German state, their cuisine, and traditional polka music, are very similar. I went for that specific reason—to reconnect with childhood pleasures. As we walked in, the band was playing the "Beer Barrel Polka" ("Roll out the barrels…"). This is a song that was very popular among Allied forces during the Second World War. It's still recognized by many people today.

Unknown to anyone in the room but me, this song was written by a Czech composer a hundred years ago. It was originally titled "Modřanská Polka," referring to my birthplace, Modřany. The neighborhood of Prague where my family lived before our forced migration. The neighborhood where we returned to spread Mother's ashes in 2018, five years after her death. My hometown.

I felt alone with this factoid. We sat at a large table and the conversation naturally turned to what brought everyone to the

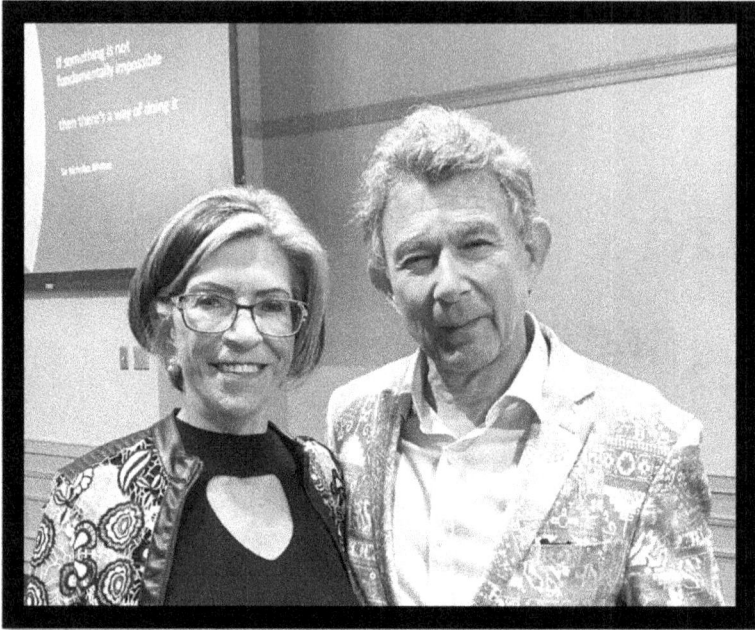

Figure 5 Legacies: Meeting Nick Winton, National Czech & Slovak Museum & Library, Cedar Rapids, Iowa, 2024. Nick's father, Sir Nicholas Winton, rescued the author's father, uncle, and 667 other Czechoslovak Jewish children from the Holocaust in 1939. In the background is a quote from Sir Nicholas: "If something is not fundamentally impossible, then there's a way of doing it."

event. A woman said her partner was from Germany. I responded that we were from "next door," Czechoslovakia.

"It's all good," she said, smiling.

"It's all good now," I laughed. Immediately I realized: this woman was in the moment, whereas I was far, far in the past—in the Second World War, the Holocaust—a time before I was even born.

The music, the beer, and the traditional food—barley soup, beef and dumplings with sour cream sauce, sauerkraut with caraway seeds—transported me in time and place. Glancing down at the table, I realized that, without my conscious awareness, I had been eating in the European style—fork in the left hand, knife in the right—rather than the American—fork in the right hand—that I typically use in the U.S. The setting and the cuisine had induced this automatic reaction. It struck me how deeply ingrained cultural practices are, how one cue can automatically elicit a host of culturally defined behaviors and feelings.

After dinner, guests got up on the dance floor to polka and my husband chatted with others. I sat, watching. This is my habit in groups. I've long thought of myself as what sociologists call the "marginal" person—the one who straddles two cultures yet is at home in neither; the one always on the edges looking in.

More than a half-century later, I am still a refugee.

George G., one of study participants, wrote in 2020, years after his interview (Grosman, 2020):

> I have built a good life. I have two amazing daughters, two amazing grandsons and a fabulous wife. I have built a good life as a jazz musician, have played many great

concerts, written fine music, met famous and interesting people. I have no complaints. And yet … and yet … Something of me was left behind as we crossed the Austrian border that fall of 1968. Something that I haven't found again. I cannot define it—but I feel a small emptiness where that something should be.

—George G., displaced at 15 in 1968.

Like George G., many of us developed highly successful careers and families. Among us are entrepreneurs, executives, professionals, artists, a U.S. Secretary of State, and a supermodel. Many of us successfully raised children who now have their own. I think we would all agree that we have been fortunate to have the opportunity to achieve the American Dream. But I also think that for most of us, our disrupted childhood is something that is never too far from our minds.

In this book, I've aimed to illustrate a more nuanced view of the immigrant success story held in the public imagination. This optimistic, grateful narrative is one that is often told by Czechoslovak refugees themselves. Yet, I've often sensed that much is left unsaid—in fact, is taboo—in such discussions. I hope that the lived experiences described here open a small window into the fuller experience of childhood forced migration.

We have seen that the journey of forced migration, especially when experienced during childhood, is a complex and multifaceted process that leaves lasting imprints on individuals and their identities. This portrayal has traversed through memories of early childhood, the often harrowing escape from a homeland, the disorienting experience of transit, and the challenges of resettlement in a foreign land. As we reach the conclusion of this exploration, several key themes emerge that highlight the enduring impact of these experiences.

Early childhood is foundational in developing a sense of trust in the world. For refugee children, the sudden loss of a familiar environment and the trauma of forced migration can profoundly disrupt this. Memories of hurried departures, perilous border crossings, and unsettling time spent in refugee camps are etched deeply into consciousness. These experiences can breed a sense of mistrust in the world—a feeling that safety is fragile and that security can be easily shattered.

The confusion and fear that accompany resettlement can lead to doubt. The struggle to navigate between two worlds—one of origin and one of refuge—often leaves us with a sense of not truly belonging anywhere. The pressure to assimilate can clash with the desire to maintain cultural practices, leading to feelings of guilt for either abandoning our roots or not fully integrating into our new society. This internal conflict is often reflected in the creation of hybrid languages like Czechlish, which serve as a bridge between two identities but also as a battleground where cultural assimilation and preservation collide.

As we move into middle adulthood, our focus shifts to contributing meaningfully to society and passing on cultural heritage to the next generation. We have grappled with the desire to preserve our cultural traditions while facing the reality that these efforts may fade as our children assimilate into the dominant culture. The narratives shared highlight the resilience and adaptability required to balance these competing demands, as well as the deep sense of responsibility felt by those who seek to pass on their heritage.

In older adulthood, we reflect on our lives and seek to find meaning and acceptance. Return journeys have served as powerful moments of reflection and reconciliation. These trips, filled with nostalgia and a longing to reconnect with a past that is both familiar and distant, highlight the complexity of bicultural identities. We find closure and peace while also struggling with feelings of alienation and regret. The ability to find meaning and acceptance in one's life journey—despite its disruptions and challenges—emerges as a central theme, underscoring the enduring impact of forced migration on the human psyche.

As we reflect on these stories, we are reminded that the experience of forced migration is not just a chapter in history but a lived reality that continues to shape lives and communities today. The experiences, challenges, and psychological impacts documented offer valuable insights for supporting displaced children today, emphasizing the importance of cultural preservation, trauma-informed support, and adaptability.

The long-term effects on identity, cultural connection, and psychological well-being evident in these stories are critical for understanding today's refugee children. Early trauma from forced migration can shape entire lives, influencing mental health, social integration, and generational continuity. Recognizing this impact can drive in long-term support for refugee children, including mental health services and educational programs that respect their heritage.

We have seen the importance of preserving cultural roots, language, and identity for refugee children adapting to new countries. Supporting community programs that nurture cultural traditions can help refugee families balance integration with preserving a sense of home and identity, promoting better long-term outcomes for children's personal development and self-esteem. The intergenerational trauma experienced by these families underscores the need for trauma-informed support services for refugees, particularly children. Schools, healthcare providers, and social services can be better equipped to support refugee families by understanding and addressing inherited trauma and providing counseling that considers family histories of war, displacement, and persecution.

We have seen how international policies, such as Cold War asylum policies, were influenced by geopolitical interests rather than humanitarian concerns alone. This historical perspective invites a re-evaluation of current refugee policies, encouraging us to prioritize human rights and the well-being of displaced people, rather than using refugee policies as tools of political influence.

Overall, the experiences of Czechoslovakia's Cold War refugee children offer valuable insights for building supportive, empathetic systems that meet the needs of today's refugee children, helping them navigate the challenges of forced migration and find belonging while preserving their cultural identities. In a world where forced migration is higher than at any time since the Second World War, the lessons learned from the past can inform how we respond to current and future refugee crises, ensuring that the dignity, identity, and well-being of displaced individuals are respected and supported.

Recommended assignments

1. Consider the causes of forced migration today. How are they similar and different from Czechoslovak forced migration during the Cold War?

2. Identify a forced migration group (national, ethnic, religious, etc.) that is seeking asylum in your country. Is your country's admissions policy toward this group generally welcoming or hostile? Does this policy trace back to Cold War refugee policies, or does it have other roots? What are the implications for future policy?

3. Conduct an oral history interview with someone who came to your country as a childhood forced migrant. Ask about their early childhood, family history, migration experience, acculturation experience, and adulthood. How has their experience impacted their life course? What did you learn about refugee children, refugee policy, future implications, or about yourself by conducting this interview?

4. Compare the experiences of Cold War-era Czechoslovak refugee children with those of refugee children from a different conflict. What similarities and differences do you see?

5. Identify one piece of knowledge you have gained from this book. How would you apply this knowledge to address today's refugee crises?

References

Boullier, M. and Blair, M. (2018). Adverse Childhood Experiences. *Paediatrics and Child Health*, 28(3), pp. 132–137. https://doi.org/10.1016/j.paed.2017.12.008

Castle, C. (2021). Language Loyalty and Language Purity in a Language Contact Situation: South Australian Czech. *Journal of Slavic Linguistics*, 29(1), pp. 1–44. https://doi.org/10.1353/jsl.2021.0000

Centropa. (2023). Asaf Auerbach. Available at: www.centropa.org/en/biography/asaf-auerbach [Accessed September 4, 2024].

Grosman, G. (2020). Fateful August Day. *Medium*. https://medium.com/@georgegrosman/fateful-august-day-e0272e0989e0

Kingery, S. (2019). Translating Spanglish to Spanish: The Brief Wondrous Life of Oscar Wao. *Translation Review*, *104*(1), 8–29. https://doi.org/10.1080/07374836.2019.1632764

Kopanic, M. J. (2022). Emigration to North America from Czechoslovakia during the Communist era. *Verbum Časopis*. Available at: https://verbumcasopis.sk/nakova/emigration-to-north-america-from-czechoslovakia-during-the-communist-era-2/ [Accessed September 4, 2024].

Lambert, J. (2018). A multitude of "lishes": The nomenclature of hybridity. *English World-Wide*, *39*(1), 1-33. https://doi.org/10.1075/eww.00001.lam

Nekola, M. (2019b). Czechs in Displaced Persons Camps. *Collegium Carolinum*. Available at: www.collegium-carolinum.de/fileadmin/Veranstaltungen/2019_Veranstaltungen/BT_Expos es_2019/2019-08-Nekola-Czech_in_Displaces_Persons_Camps.pdf [Accessed September 4, 2024].

Nekola, M. (2022). Czechoslovak Refugees in the Displaced Persons Camps in the Early Cold War. *The Exile History Review*, (1), pp. 25–35. Available at: https://czasopisma.kul.pl/index.php/ehr/article/view/14614 [Accessed September 4, 2024].

Palovic, Z. and Bereghazyova, G. (2020). *Czechoslovakia: Behind the Iron Curtain*. Slovakia: Global Slovakia.

Prucha, E. (2018). Raising Children Who Speak Czechlish. *Half 'n Half.* https://halfnhalf-life.com/2018/02/02/raising-children-who-speak-czechlish/

Raska, F. D. (2012). *The Long Road to Victory: A History of Czechoslovak Exile Organizations after 1968.* New York: Columbia University Press.

Raska, J. (2018). *Czech Refugees in Cold War Canada: 1945–1989.* Winnipeg: University of Manitoba Press.

Rumbaut, R. G. (2004). Ages, Life Stages, and Generational Cohorts: Decomposing the Immigrant First and Second Generations in the United States. *International Migration Review*, 38(3), pp. 1160–1205. https://doi.org/10.1111/j.1747-7379.2004.tb00232.x

Sparling, D., Simona, K. and Rance, C. (2021). *English or Czenglish*. Brno, Czech Republic: Masaryk University.

U.S. Citizenship and Immigration Service. (2023). *Refugee Timeline*. Available at: www.uscis.gov/about-us/our-history/history-office-and-library/featured-stories-from-the-uscis-history-office-and-library/refugee-timeline [Accessed September 4, 2024].

U.S. Holocaust Museum. (2021). Lidice: The Annihilation of a Czech Town. Holocaust Encyclopedia. https://encyclopedia.ushmm.org/content/en/article/lidice.

Weisskirch, R. S. (2010). Child Language Brokers in Immigrant Families: An Overview of Family Dynamics. *MediAzioni*, 10(1), pp. 68–87. http://mediazioni.sitlec.unibo.it/. ISSN 1974-4382.

Zolberg, A. R. (1988). The Roots of American Refugee Policy. *Social Research*, pp. 649–678. www.jstor.org/stable/40970524

Czech
out these movies

An American Rhapsody (2001): In 1950, a Hungarian couple is forced to flee from the oppressive communist country for the USA with their eldest daughter, but are forced to leave behind their infant daughter Suzanne (Scarlett Johansson) who is raised by a kindly foster couple. Six years later, Peter and Margit arrange for the American Red Cross to bring Suzanne to their new home in Los Angeles where the perplexed youth is forced to accept her sudden change in home and country which leads to a troubled growing up. At age 15, the rebellious and unsure-of-herself Suzanne tries to come to terms with her roots and decides to travel back to Budapest, Hungary to find her true identity (1h 46 m; streaming).

Europe's Forgotten Border (2022): During the Cold War, the border between Czechoslovakia and the West became a dramatic scene. Between 1945 and 1989 several hundred people lost their lives. Thirty years after the fall of the Iron Curtain, justice is now to be served: German and Czech public prosecutors are trying to bring the truth to light. The film reconstructs the events through the eyes of perpetrators, victims, bereaved families and those responsible (52m; streaming).

One Life (2023): The true story of Sir Nicholas "Nicky" Winton (Sir Anthony Hopkins), a young London broker who, in the months leading up to Second World War, rescued 669 predominantly Jewish children from the Nazis. Nicky visited

Prague in December 1938 and found families who had fled the rise of the Nazis in Germany and Austria, living in desperate conditions with little or no shelter and food, and under threat of Nazi invasion. He immediately realized it was a race against time. How many children could he and the team rescue before the borders closed? Fifty years later, it's 1988 and Nicky lives haunted by the fate of the children he wasn't able to bring to safety in England; always blaming himself for not doing more. It's not until a live BBC television show, "That's Life", surprises him by introducing him to some surviving children—now adults—that he finally begins to come to terms with the guilt and grief he had carried for five decades (1h 50m; streaming).

Winton—From Prague to Penkhull With Love (2017). This documentary carries interviews with four "Winton Children" (including my late uncle, Asaf Auerbach) as they returned to Stoke-on-Trent, England, 70 years after they were rescued from Czechoslovakia and brought to the Penkhull Children's Homes there (35m; www.youtube.com/watch?v=vBve_2qd frc&t=1700s).

80 years apart (2017). These are the real stories of Harry and Ahmed, told in their own words. Though generations separate them, there are unsettling parallels between their stories as child refugees (2m; www.youtube.com/watch?v=PTk7 a1s8vR8).

Participant biographies

(Original Czech or Slovak names included where available)

Alex Vesely (Aleš Veselý) was born in Příbram (today's Czechia), in 1966. His father worked as a mine foreman, and his mother held an office job. In 1983, when Alex was 17, his mother decided to emigrate with her children and her second husband. The family escaped while on vacation in Yugoslavia, spending several months in a Belgrade refugee camp before settling in Chicago. Alex worked in construction and as a sculptor. He was interviewed in 2010 at age 44.

Barbara Reinfeld (Barbora Koháková) was born in Prague in 1935. Her father was a journalist, and her mother a former English teacher. Both parents were imprisoned in concentration camps during WWII for their resistance activities. They survived and returned to Prague. Following the Communist coup, the family escaped to Germany, where they stayed in the Regensburg refugee camp, followed by a year in Munich before ultimately settling in New York City. Barbara earned a doctorate in Czech history from Columbia University and taught history at the university level for over 25 years. She was interviewed in 2012 at age 77 and passed away in 2020 at 84.

Charles Heller (Ota Heller) was born in Prague in 1936. His father owned a clothing firm seized by the Nazis during WWII, leading his father to flee in 1940. In 1944, his mother was sent to a labor camp, and Charles hid on a family friend's farm. Reunited with his parents in 1945, the family fled Prague after their property was nationalized. They settled in New Jersey, where Charles attended Oklahoma State University on a basketball scholarship, becoming an engineer and venture capitalist. He was interviewed in 2010 at age 74.

Dagmar Benedik (Dagmar Verflová) was born in Kladno (today's Czechia) in 1952. Her father was a hockey coach, and her mother was a teacher. In 1968, when Dagmar was 16, the family planned a vacation to Germany but left Czechoslovakia permanently after the Warsaw Pact invasion. They spent weeks in the Karlsruhe refugee camp before moving to Toronto. In 1995, she returned to Prague to work as a translator and stayed for six years. Dagmar was interviewed in 2011 at age 59.

Duke (Edward) Dellin was born in Prague in 1940. His father studied agricultural engineering and later became involved in politics as the Secretary of the Czechoslovak Agrarian Party. After the Communist coup in 1948, his father fled to Paris, and Duke's mother soon followed with Duke and his sister. The family eventually arrived in the United States, where Duke later worked in investment banking. He was interviewed in 2010 at age 70 and passed away in 2021 at age 81.

Emil Brlit was born in 1954 in Nitra, Slovakia. His father was a dentist and his mother a dental assistant. Following the 1948 Communist coup, his father's practice was nationalized. In 1969, when Emil was 15, the family moved to Austria, staying with relatives before eventually settling in Chicago. Emil owned dental laboratories and was interviewed in 2013 at age 59.

George Drost was born in Brno in 1946. His father was a lawyer, and his mother was a homemaker. Following the Communist coup in 1948, George's father fled the country, with his family joining him two years later. They eventually moved to Chicago, where George became an attorney in private practice. He was interviewed in 2011 at age 65.

George Grosman (Jiří Grosman) was born in Prague in 1953. His parents were Holocaust survivors.His mother worked as a biologist and his father as a screenwriter. After the 1968 invasion, the family emigrated to Tel Aviv, where George studied English literature and linguistics. He later moved to London and then to Toronto, where he worked as a musician. George was interviewed in 2011 at age 58.

George Heller (Jiří Heller) was born in Mariánské Lázně (today's Czechia) in 1948. His parents owned a bakery. After the Communist coup, they emigrated to Israel and eventually settled in Montréal. George began working for Hudson's Bay Company and rose to become CEO in 1999. He was interviewed in 2011 at age 63.

Hana Voris (Hana Voříšková) was born in Písek (today's Czechia) in 1947. After the Communist coup, her father left Czechoslovakia, with Hana and her mother following soon after. The family settled in Cleveland, Ohio, where Hana studied French and Russian. She spent five years in Prague following the Velvet Revolution working as an English teacher. After returning to Cleveland, she worked as an English teacher for refugees. She was interviewed in 2010 at age 63.

Ivana Edwards (Ivana Šmejkalová) was born in Prague in 1946. Her mother owned a perfume shop, and her father ran a leather business. In 1949, the family fled to Israel before settling in Montréal. Ivana pursued a journalism career and traveled frequently to Prague after the Velvet Revolution. She was interviewed in 2011 at age 65.

Jerri Zbiral (Jaroslava Zbíralová) was born in Prague in 1948. Her mother survived the Lidice tragedy and endured years in Ravensbrück concentration camp. After the Communist coup, the family emigrated to Germany, then Norway, and ultimately Montréal. Jerri became an art dealer specializing in Czech photography. She was interviewed in 2010 at age 62.

Jerry Rabas (Jaroslav Rabas) was born in Pardubice (today's Czechia) in 1945. His family fled Czechoslovakia in 1948 following political warnings against his father. After spending time in refugee camps, they settled in Chicago, where Jerry owned a travel agency specializing in travel to Czechoslovakia. He was interviewed in 2010 at age 65 and passed away in 2013 at age 68.

Joan Zizek (Jana Rabasová) was born in Pardubice (today's Czechia) in 1941. After her father was warned of his arrest, the family fled Czechoslovakia, spending time in refugee camps before settling in Chicago. She was interviewed in 2010 at age 69.

Karol Sith was born in Bratislava in 1983. His mother was a nurse and his father was a mechanical engineer. The family emigrated in 1986, first to Yugoslavian refugee camps and then to Austria before settling in Fox Lake, Illinois. Karol studied aviation administration at Lewis University. He was interviewed in 2011 at age 28.

Lucia Maruska (Lucia Marušková) was born in Cífer (today's Slovakia) in 1953. Her father was an accountant, and her mother managed a knitting factory. Lucia's father escaped communist Czechoslovakia when she was nine, and after four years of legal struggles, the family joined him in Los Angeles. Lucia studied art history and often returned to Slovakia. She was interviewed in 2011 at age 58 and passed away in 2015 at 61.

Luke Vanis (Lukáš Vaniš) was born in Prague in 1971. His mother was a teacher and designerand his father taught art. After his parents divorced, his mother took him to Yugoslavia, where they sought asylum. The family spent time in Austria before settling near Chicago. Luke became a freelance designer and photographer. He was interviewed in 2012 at age 41.

Madeleine Albright (Marie Jana Korbelová) was born in Prague in 1937. Her father was a diplomat in the Czechoslovak Foreign Ministry. The family moved to Britain during WWII before returning to Prague after the war. Following the Communist coup in 1948, the family sought asylum in the United States and settled in Denver. Madeleine earned a doctorate from Columbia University. . During the Clinton administration, she served first as Ambassador to the United Nations and then as Secretary of State. She was interviewed in 2013 at age 76 and died in 2022 at 84.

Michlean Amir (Michlean Lowy) was born in France in 1940 to Czech Jewish parents. During WWII, the family lived in England and later returned to Czechoslovakia. After the Communist coup, they emigrated to Israel before moving to Rochester, New York. Michlean worked as an archivist at the United States Holocaust Memorial Museum. She was interviewed in 2011 at age 71.

Paul Burik (Pavel Burik) was born in České Budějovice (today's Czechia) in 1954. His father was a doctor, and his mother was a pharmacist. After the 1968 invasion, they emigrated to the United States and settled in Cleveland, where Paul worked as an architect. He was interviewed in 2010 at age 56.

Paulina Porizkova (Pavlína Pořízková) was born in Olomouc (today's Czechia) in 1965. Her parents emigrated after the 1968 invasion, leaving her with her grandparents. The family reunited several years later in Sweden. At 15, Paulina signed with Elite Models and moved to Paris to begin a modeling career. She became a supermodel and actress in the 1980s and later an author. She was interviewed in 2013 at age 47.

Pavel Paces (Pavel Pačes) was born in Prague in 1949. His father owned a liquor distillery and his mother was the office manager for the business. His family fled shortly after his birth, as his father faced arrest by the Communists for resistance activities. After a month in hiding, the family reunited in New York City, where Pavel studied education and became an industrial arts teacher. He was interviewed in 2012 at age 63.

Peter Esterle was born in Bratislava in 1973. His father was a meteorologist, and his mother worked for IBM. In 1980, the family used a vacation to Yugoslavia as an opportunity to escape, eventually settling in Milwaukee. Peter studied electrical engineering and worked in controls engineering. He was interviewed in 2011 at age 38.

Petra Sith was born in Bratislava in 1979. Her family emigrated after spending time in Yugoslavian and Austrian refugee camps, settling in Fox Lake, Illinois. Petra graduated from Roosevelt University and worked as a billing processor. She was interviewed in 2010 at age 31.

Rudy (Rudolf) Solfronk was born in Žinkovy (today's Czechia) in 1935. His family left Czechoslovakia when his father faced arrest after refusing to give up his farm. They settled in Cicero,

Illinois, where Rudy worked as a print shop foreman. He was interviewed in 2010 at age 75.

Savoy Horvath was born in Brno (today's Czechia) in 1933. In 1948, at age 15, he fled to Germany after helping Yugoslav friends escape, eventually moving to the United States. Savoy worked as a sheet metal fabricator in Chicago. He was interviewed in 2011 at age 78 and died in 2015 at age 82.

Susan Lucak was born in Teplice (today's Czechia) in 1955. Her father was an orchestra conductor, and her mother was a teacher. The family left Czechoslovakia following the 1968 invasion and settled in New York City, where Susan became a gastroenterologist. She was interviewed in 2012 at age 57.

Thomas Hasler (Tomáš Hašler) was born in Prague in 1941. His father, a popular Czech songwriter, was arrested and murdered by the Gestapo. In 1949, Thomas and his mother fled to Australia and later moved to the United States. Thomas earned a master's degree and worked as a journalist. He was interviewed in 2011 at age 70 and passed away in 2023 at age 82.

Tony Jandacek (Antonín Jandáček) was born in Prague in 1934. His father, a journalist, fled after the Communist coup. The family eventually reunited in Chicago, where Tony became a Czech teacher and interpreter. He was interviewed in 2010 at age 76 and died in 2022 at age 87.

Vaclav Slovak (Václav Slovák) was born in Šumperk (today's Czechia) in 1956. His family emigrated to Austria after their restaurant was subjected to scrutiny by the Communist regime, eventually settling in Atlanta. Vaclav studied electrical engineering at Georgia Tech. He was interviewed in 2011 at age 55.

Valentin Turansky (Valentin Turánský) was born in Stupava (today's Slovakia) in 1938. His family fled to Austria after his father's imprisonment for refusing to incorporate his small farm into the local cooperative. He spent six months in prison, and was then sentenced to a further six months of forced labor, which he spent working in a coal mine. Upon his release in 1952, the Turansky family decided to leave the country. They ultimately settled in Chicago, where Valentin worked in a print shop. He was interviewed in 2011 at age 73.

Vladimir Maule was born in Prague in 1952. His father was a part-owner of a high-end hotel. Vladimir and his mother fled following the 1968 invasion. They settled in Chicago, where Vladimir studied film and became owner of a film production company. He was interviewed in 2010 at age 58.

Yvette Kaiser-Smith (Yveta Kaiserová) was born in Prague in 1958. Her father, working in theater, decided to bring the family to the U.S. after the 1968 invasion. They settled in Dallas, where Yvette earned an MFA and became an artist. She was interviewed in 2012 at age 54.

Index

www.ingramcontent.com/pod-product-compliance
Lightning Source LLC
Chambersburg PA
CBHW070350270326
41926CB00017B/4069